the
LIFE READY
woman

the
LIFE READY
woman

Thriving in a Do-It-All World

SHAUNTI FELDHAHN & ROBERT LEWIS

B&H
PUBLISHING GROUP
Nashville, Tennessee

978-1-4336-7112-8

Published by B&H Publishing Group
Nashville, Tennessee

Dewey Decimal Classification: 248.843
Subject Heading: CHRISTIAN LIFE / WOMEN

Scripture taken from the New American Standard Bible, copyright
© 1960, 1962, 1963, 1968, 1971, 1972, 1973, 1975, 1977, 1995 by The
Lockman Foundation. Used by permission.

Also used: New International Version (NIV), copyright © 1973, 1978,
1984 by International Bible Society.

Also used: New Living Translation (NLT), copyright 1996, 2004.
Used by permission of Tyndale House Publishers, Inc., Wheaton,
Illinois 60189. All rights reserved.

2 3 4 5 6 7 • 15 14 13 12 11

From Shaunti

To a husband and children who have helped me live out my callings, have forgiven me when I have gotten it wrong, and show me the loving heart of God every day.

From Robert

To women everywhere who are bold enough to trust Jesus Christ with their lives and their priorities. Eternity belongs to you.

Contents

Introduction
Being Life Ready

$\mathcal{A}$nita woke up at 6:00 a.m. Normally she would lie in bed and think, pray, and plan until Ron awoke, but not today. For weeks, *months*, this day had crowded everything else out of her mind. But enough with thinking. It was time to move.

After a quick shower she dressed and headed for the kitchen. She paused to peek inside her children's rooms, with a nostalgic smile for the empty beds. When the kids were young, she had negotiated a part-time arrangement with her boss so she could be with them as much as possible. Motherhood then had been about monsters under the bed, scraped knees, Big Wheels, bedtime stories, and the never-ending question: "Why, Mommy?" Later it became endless carpools, schoolwork, athletic events, and volatile boy-girl relationships. Anita had been there for it all, having put a fast-track career on "slow" for a while to do so. She'd do it all again in a heartbeat. There were no regrets except that this time had passed. The kids were in college now, and she had reengaged her career full time five years ago. She could hardly believe how events had unfolded to lead up to this day.

As Anita set the coffeemaker in motion, the business of the day rushed back upon her. More than one amazing event was unfolding right now. She smiled at the tension in her stomach, then turned on the TV at the breakfast bar to catch news about her sister. Select polls had been open for more than an hour now; newscasters were poring over anemic streams of data, somehow converting them into "scientific" predictions on how the day would unfold. "Joanna Taylor is sure to win the Senate seat," said one pollster. "No, no, this thing is still up for grabs," countered another. Anita tried not to listen, but she couldn't think of not listening. "Go, Jo, go!" she breathed.

"How's she doing?" Ron asked as he came into the kitchen.

"Far too early to say," Anita replied. "It's silly of me to be watching."

"Not at all," Ron said as he drew up next to her and gave a reassuring hug.

"I've got to get going," Anita said, quickly refocusing on the day's big events. "I'll swing by the poll and vote—*several times* if I can," she laughed. "Then I'm meeting Sandy at 10:00 for a final walk-through of the merger contract. And I promised Emily I'd squeeze in a quick lunch about her GED exam."

Ron shook his head in admiration. "You're something, you know that? Today your sister's set to become a U.S. senator, you're closing one of the biggest deals your company has ever made, and still you make time for the teenage mother you're mentoring. What else can you fit into this day? Hey, the driveway needs resealing," he suggested with a wry smile.

Anita laughed as she finished off a muffin and turned to pick up her laptop bag.

Ron stopped her for a moment by putting his hands on her shoulders. "Just be home in time for us to enjoy this night together, okay?"

"You got it," Anita answered firmly. Then, with a sigh of reflection, she paused and said, "Ron, think about what this day means." A photograph, framed in red, sat atop the counter in front of her. She turned it so Ron could see. It was Anita's great-grandmother. "Grandma Parry never saw a day like this. She was smart and ambitious, but she never set foot in a college. She never held a job that paid real money either, let alone run for an elected office! Yet in many ways all the opportunities that Jo and I have are owed to her and others like her. Maybe by giving both of us such big moments on the same day, God is reminding us how privileged we are."

Ron nodded. "Well, by tonight I'll have a senator in the family and a record-setting businesswoman who is launching others into the future. Great day to be a Parry woman!"

"A great day to be a *woman*," Anita corrected him. She righted the picture frame, blew Ron a kiss, and stepped out into a world of opportunity that her great-grandmother could never have imagined.

Looking Forward

It *is* a great day to be a woman. The choices and opportunities available to women in the twenty-first century are amazing—opportunities that could never have been imagined one hundred years ago. Yet we also encounter challenges that our great-grandmothers could never have fathomed.

Every woman knows the feeling of struggling to juggle and balance everything and watching our friends and loved ones do the same. Every woman has looked at the clock and lamented that there just aren't enough hours in the day. And every woman has also enjoyed the wonderful opportunities God provides us that simply didn't exist just a few generations ago. The trick is to know *how* to manage this crazy, modern life. And for those of us who are followers of Jesus, to know how to manage our modern life from a biblical perspective rather than an ever-changing cultural one.

> There is a way to be "ready" for today's modern life in a way that leads to peace and enjoyment rather than stress and regret.

The good news is: there is a way to do this! There is a way to be "ready" for today's modern life in a way that leads to peace and enjoyment rather than stress and regret. There is a way to help other women do so, too. No matter how crazy your life is, there is a solid, encouraging, and empowering guide that we can find in the ancient words of the Bible that applies directly to our life today as contemporary women. And no matter where you are—younger, older; single, married, divorced, remarried;

stay-at-home mom or busy executive; no matter your ethnic background or even your personal faith beliefs or questions—you can start today to reach for it.

Becoming "Life Ready" will require thinking purposefully about subjects you may never have thought through before. It will require courageous steps of faith at some points and waiting for open doors in others. But the end result will be that you not only survive but thrive in our do-it-all world. Actually *being* a Life Ready Woman means that you are clear about your life, bold in your faith, and able to find God's best for *you*.

This book is intimately connected to a video series by the same name. You definitely don't need the video series in order to go through the book, but if you are reading the book before engaging with the video experience, we encourage you to go through that as your next step, either alone or—even better—with a group, as it will help walk you through the process of creating a personal application to your life. If you are reading the book *during* the video series, or as a follow-up to it, we encourage you to use this material to go even more in-depth as you walk through your own personal application.

This book is broken down into two distinct parts. The first five chapters—part 1—are about God's desired context for our lives. In these chapters we will explicitly identify the mold that the world tries to fit us into (which we often aren't even aware of!) and contrast that with the amazing design and callings that God created for us. As women, we'll take a look at what many of us might subconsciously believe about femininity and womanhood (not our "roles" but what it means to *be* a woman) and contrast it with what God has to say. We'll talk about what might be keeping you from the life you're longing to live. **Part 1 of the book will culminate with chapter 5, the most foundational chapter in the book, which will help you discover the big-picture callings God has for your life**—*big-picture callings that set the stage for everything else.*

In part 2 you will see how you, personally, can thrive in a do-it-all world. How are you individually designed? What do your unique callings and circumstances mean for how you arrange your life? And what steps of faith do you need to take in order to reach God's best? These chapters will take us from the big-picture context to one that is personal and get you started on the path. And then, as noted, we encourage those of you who want to move to detailed personal application to go through the *Life Ready Woman* video series.

A Personal Note

Before we dive in, let us explain who "we" are. Two people are writing this book: Shaunti Feldhahn and Robert Lewis. I (Shaunti) have become a best-selling author and speaker over the years, but I am also a wife and mom who balances this crazy modern life every day—and as a woman, much of this book will be written in my voice. Robert is a long-time leader in the Christian community, former senior pastor of the large Fellowship Bible Church in Little Rock, and is producing a number of *Life Ready* video resources, including *The Life Ready Woman*. He authored the original book (*The New Eve*) that led to this one, which in turn arose out of his experience as the founder of a nationwide movement called Men's Fraternity.

The hundreds of thousands of men packing into early-morning Men's Fraternity Bible studies across the country are being attracted by a similar desire for a biblical vision: a model for what it means to be a godly, biblically guided man in a culture that no longer agrees on what that ideal looks like—or whether it is even necessary. Men's Fraternity offers a model that men can measure their personal and professional life by . . . and change it if it doesn't measure up.

Well, ladies, it is our turn. Many of us try to live a godly life and follow the Bible's specific precepts. But without ever intending to, we could still be making choices that are at odds with how God has designed us. To the extent we do, we will have regret instead of contentment. And we will drastically limit our ability to be good stewards of the gifts God has given us, leaving us unsatisfied and hindering the purpose for which God gave us those gifts. But to the extent that we live in accordance with God's design and callings for us, we'll thrive.

Regardless of where you are in life, we hope this book will give you a modern, encouraging vision for what it means to be a godly, biblically guided woman in the twenty-first century. In an era where women rightfully have high expectations personally and professionally, and *can* do almost anything we set our minds to, this model will help us navigate what we *should*—and should not do.

> To the extent that we live in accordance with God's design and callings for us, we'll thrive. ❧

I (Shaunti) see how profoundly this model has helped me. As some of you might guess, I'm extremely busy both professionally and personally. As noted, I'm an author, researcher, and traveling speaker; but I'm also a wife and mom to two young children. I try to be a supportive wife to my husband's entrepreneurial business, but I also have my own.

And privately, for years, I have been torn by how to balance it all, how to keep all the plates spinning. With this biblical blueprint, I finally feel like I have a clear and realistic model that I can look up to and respect as a modern Christian woman, something that can help me make the decisions that will lead to relief, delight, and fulfillment instead of regret.

That doesn't mean those decisions are easy. For me it has meant a willingness to reexamine some professional opportunities in light of personal ones. For others it may mean examining whether you are fully using your unique God-given gifts for the impact He intends you to have. But once you make these decisions, they will *fit*. You will feel like you are finally functioning in the ways for which you were designed.

Be willing to be challenged, sister! The end result will be worth it.

PART 1

❧

God's Plan and Purposes for All of Us

1

I Am Woman

*I*magine for a moment that one of your favorite female Bible characters were to somehow travel through time to the modern day. What would Esther, or Ruth, or Mary Magdaline think as they stared, amazed, at our lives? Sure, their immediate focus would be on the marvels of washing machines, telephones, and airplanes. But I think something else would strike a far deeper and more personal chord: what a woman's life looks like today. Because to them, the opportunities we have and the power we wield in our culture would look astonishing.

The straight fact is that we as women have more power—personally, professionally, and politically—than at any other time in human history. And that power trajectory is predicted to rise even further in the decades to come. "Women will rock," predicts Ron Fournier, author of *Applebee's America*. Today they "are getting better grades, running a majority of student governments, and graduating from college in larger numbers than their male counterparts."[1] (Girls, in fact, are doing so well in school compared to their often-struggling male counterparts, that analysts like me believe we now need to provide more encouragement to boys!)

Celinda Lake and Kellyanne Conway in their research see that a major cultural transition has taken place. They write, "Without fanfare, almost stealthily, America has become women-centric. . . . Women—from seniors to boomers to Generations X and Y—are recasting the nation in their image" and "shaking the culture to its core."[2]

These statements are especially breathtaking when one remembers how far women have come in such a short time. Fewer than one hundred years ago, *we couldn't even vote!* Our opportunities, as compared to men's, were extremely limited. For many millennia a woman's world was controlled and defined primarily by her husband and home.

But then new winds began to blow. Changes in the law expanded our horizons. Women won the right to vote (by *one vote*) in 1920 and gained a new voice and powerful influence in shaping society. Growing educational opportunities opened up a woman's mind to new possibilities. The advent of World War II gave thousands of women new experiences. Many discovered they could do "a man's job" by working in factories and running assembly lines, building and flying airplanes, managing businesses, and constructing the war machine their men unleashed half a world away.

After the war, technology opened up a woman's time. Chores that once took hours were now finished with the touch of a button. A woman's schedule was now freer than ever before for "something more." But what?

Finally, the feminist movement of the latter decades of the twentieth century opened up a woman's opportunities like no movement had before it. Women no longer *had to* stay quiet, stay at home, or stay trapped by certain systemic injustices. Of course, as with so many huge societal shifts, these liberating changes also came with a dark side; promising freedom or choices that in reality delivered heartache for women, families, and society. But, indisputably, this time period also opened up opportunities and eliminated long-standing inequities.

And to the degree that society balked at either aspect of this transition, women were there en masse to confront the culture (in both healthy and unhealthy ways) and change it. "I am woman, hear me roar!" Helen Reddy sang as newly liberated women broke into male-dominated public domains, overturned rigid social structures, and took new ground for ever-growing ambitions.

Regardless of how we got here, in the twenty-first century, women have more rights, choices, and freedoms than ever before. While there are still some areas women haven't cracked in large numbers (like the top levels of corporate America), in many arenas we are not only moving toward equality with men but are even surpassing our male counterparts. (See chart below for examples.)

Workforce. Half of the American workforce is female. And from 1950 to the present day, the percentage of women in the workforce has at least doubled in every age category over the age of twenty-five. For example, the Bureau of Labor Statistics shows that among women age thirty-five to forty-four, just 39 percent worked in 1950. By 1998, that number was 77 percent.[3]

Earnings Gap. In 1979, full-time female employees earned only 62 percent of what men earned, compared to 83 percent in 2010—still not equal, but improving. And in 2010, single women under thirty earned 8 percent more on average than their male counterparts.[4]

Working Moms / Dual-Income Families. In 1975, 47 percent of mothers with children under eighteen held jobs, compared to 71 percent in 2009. Further, in 2009, more than 77 percent of women with kids age six to seventeen years old held jobs, three out of four of them full time. In 1997, 66 percent of married and partnered employees lived in dual-income families. By 2008, this had increased to 79 percent. Additionally, in 2008, 26 percent of women in dual-income families earned at least 10 percent more than their spouses or partners, an increase from 15 percent in 1997.[5]

Breadwinning. In 1970, women contributed less than 6 percent of family income. Today, the "typical working wife" contributes 42 percent. And four out of ten mothers (largely single mothers) are the primary breadwinners for their family.[6]

Business Ownership. In 2008, 40 percent of all privately held firms had 50 percent or more female ownership. In that year, 10.1 million firms were owned 75 percent or more by women. Those businesses employed more than 13 million people and generated $1.9 trillion in sales.[7]

Business Management. A 2007 research study showed that Fortune 500 companies with three or more women on their board of directors outperformed companies with fewer female board members by as much as 66 percent. While the highest levels of corporate America remain overwhelmingly male (usually at least 85 percent), the pipeline for the first time poises women with a good chance to crack the glass ceiling.[8]

Church Involvement and Lay Leadership. After a nationwide survey, George Barna concluded, "Women shoulder most of the responsibility for the health and vitality of the Christian faith in the United States."[9]

Education. From kindergarten to graduate school, females are achieving far more than males, so much so that one leading publication says males are now the "second sex."[10]

College Enrollment. In the fall of 2008, 55 percent of college students were female.[11] That's a stunning turnaround from the 1960s, when 66 percent of college students were male. Furthermore, female students are 33 percent more likely to graduate than their male counterparts.[12] *The New York Times* summed it up this way in a front-page headline: "At Colleges, Women Are Leaving Men in the Dust." *The Times* went on to say, "Academically, boys are about where they were thirty years ago, but girls are just on a tear, doing much, much better."[13]

Bachelor's Degrees. In fields of study ranging from biology to business, history to social science, and psychology to education, women are earning the majority of college degrees.[14] Almost 60 percent of all bachelor's degrees today are awarded to women.[15]

Master's Degrees. In 2007, women earned more than 60 percent of all master's degrees[16] and comprise 35 percent of all students in MBA programs.[17]

Professional Degrees. In 1971, women earned only 6 percent of professional degrees (such as medical and law degrees). By 2005, the percentage had soared to 50 percent.[18]

In fact, in certain arenas of women's advancement, the pendulum appears not to be settling at a comfortable equity between men and women but to be swinging too far in the other direction. All of the statistics in the sidebar are revealing, but the ones concerning education are especially telling because education is one of the best predictors of future demographics.

As former U.S. Secretary of Education Margaret Spellings described it, the fact of the female majority on college campuses alone "has profound implications for the economy, society, families, and democracy."[19] In a July 2010 cover story in the magazine *The Atlantic,* Hanna Rosin explained, "More than ever, college is the gateway to economic success," in not just the upper-middle class but the middle class as well. She concluded, "It's this broad, striving middle class that defines our society. And demographically, we can see with absolute clarity that in the coming decades the middle class will be dominated by women."

As this enormous social realignment plays out, men will—and already are—increasingly finding themselves tailoring their lives to women (for example, working for a female boss or being the secondary breadwinner at home) rather than vice versa. How far that restructuring will extend is an open question. (For example, in business, upper management looks likely to continue its male majority.) And whether men, women, and society will adapt well and arrest the overcorrection of the pendulum remains to be seen. But regardless, the restructuring is coming—and in many cases is well underway.

A Warning from History

God created men and women equal and *wants* women to experience equality with men. Freedom, power, and opportunity are wonderful assets. Yet thousands of years of history shows more of that dark side that can occur when newly won rights and freedoms are not handled well. In his book *Caesar and Christ,* Will Durant detailed one prime example of this from the first two centuries AD, when women in the major urban centers of the Roman Empire experienced their own season of liberation. Indeed, the parallels to our present day make ancient Rome feel like America's historical twin.

That's because Roman women of this era had also acquired new and expanded freedoms that went well beyond the traditional boundaries. Long held back by law and custom, they won unprecedented rights for themselves and in many cases even a level playing field with men. Where they gained new power, they became doctors and lawyers, owned property, and traded goods. They enjoyed the liberty of conducting business with men in private quarters. This new tang of freedom was exhilarating, dizzying—and seductive.

As is the temptation for anyone tasting freedom for the first time, wisdom and restraint soon became the enemies of freedom rather than guidance for it. Excess and foolishness (disguised as chic living) became the new virtues. Women (like many men in an increasingly loose society) shunned modesty and wore however little they liked. Adulteries increased so much as to deaden the sense of scandal. Divorce was common; open marriage was more so. Men preferred concubines to wives, and wives sought lovers in full view of their husbands. Abortion became a mundane means of birth control. Women lobbied for and eventually won the right to fight alongside men in military combat roles. Classic femininity became decidedly out of vogue in the new Rome. With this new femininity and the shift from an agrarian to a cosmopolitan social structure, women pursued new, more aggressive roles in society and, along with their husbands, gave less and less attention to their homes.

Does any of this sound familiar?

Predictably, family problems exploded and birthrates fell sharply. Childbearing interrupted opportunity and the pursuit of beauty, so women actively avoided it. Caesar Augustus was so alarmed at these developments that he moved to bolster the image of motherhood in Rome by according mothers special honor in public. He dressed them in fine robes, exempted them from taxes, seated them in the luxury boxes at the Colosseum, and earnestly bid the nation do homage to the institute of motherhood. But his bid failed. The new Roman woman simply wasn't interested.[20]

In a final reflection on Rome's gender revolution, Durant noted that these women in their liberty chose more often than not to emulate men's *vices* rather than their virtues. Perhaps more to the point, Roman women took their new equality with men as an opportunity to become virtually indistinguishable from the men they once chafed under and disdained.[21] And today I've noticed a similar dynamic in my own research with women and men in the corporate marketplace for my recent book *The Male Factor*. Many male executives told me how ironic it was that some talented women incorrectly felt like they had to "be like a man" to succeed—since they usually ended up taking on the *worst* attributes of men—those obnoxious characteristics that men said they even disliked about each other.[22]

The freedoms and opportunities women have gained in this past century are wonderful, and we should be overwhelmingly grateful to see women excelling in so many areas. However, history shows that the freedom to excel can also lead to the freedom to bind oneself to greater evils and new sorrows.

You might think, *well that doesn't sound like me*. Really? How about a different way of saying much the same thing? The freedom to excel can also lead us to take on burdens we were never meant to carry, to find ourselves stressed and torn, and to experience an outlook that is all too often marked by worry or guilt instead of the absolute peace of knowing we are in the exact center of God's will every day.

Does that sound more familiar?

The reality is that all of us—both women and men—have experienced the downside of today's life of freedom and opportunity. And we all need to guard ourselves from taking our freedoms in directions we were never meant to go.

How Do We Do That?

It sounds so simple to "guard ourselves"—and yet in real life, it is so difficult to do. As modern women, we have an endless option of choices in front of us every single day. While some day-to-day or big-picture life choices come with clear "steer clear!" road signs that anyone can see (although not everyone obeys), many other paths look benign, even appealing at the start. Yet while some choices will end up being good or neutral, others will end up being bad or even disastrous.

Even more confusing, sometimes, is the reality that a path that would end up disastrous for you might in fact be God's perfectly designed path for some other person. That is not relativism. It is the reality that God has a unique design and calling for every person He has lovingly created. As Paul's letter to the Ephesians puts it, each of us were "created in Christ Jesus to do good works, which God prepared in advance for us to do" (2:10).

So how do you discover God's best for *you*? Where is the help that can cut through the fog to help you decide how to live smart and well? I think all of us would agree that God *wants* us to find His best for us. He wants us to be what the Life Ready theme summarizes: women who are clear about our lives, bold in our faith, and able to find God's best for us! But the question is *how* we do that.

Unfortunately, today there is a lack of discipleship and "life coaching" (the kind mentioned in Titus 2) that offers trustworthy navigational guidelines to assist women in discerning which choices are best and which, however alluring, might be empty promises or tragic dead ends. All of this leaves women asking, "How do I know on the front end which choices deliver the most out of life? And how do I avoid major mistakes and lifelong disappointments?" Such are the questions constantly circling around our lives today, especially whenever big life choices have to be made.

> God *wants* us to find His best for us. ॐ

As I (Shaunti) was exploring how different women might tackle these "how" questions, I pulled together a core discussion group of fourteen Christian women of different backgrounds, ages, ethnic groups, and life paths. This group served as my small group to help me think through and develop the *Life Ready Woman* video series on this subject. One of this group, a twenty-five-year-old named Julia, put into words exactly the thrill that many women feel in the modern era—although perhaps not as acutely at some times as at others. As Julia said, "I have just graduated from college, and the whole world is out there in front of me with all of these choices. I don't know how to decide, and I don't even know what is best for me, how to decide what's best for me, or which path to take. . . . I just don't know. I just don't know!"

As Caitlin Flanagan said, "The unpleasant truth [is] that life presents a series of choices, each of which precludes a host of other attractive possibilities."[23] What adds additional anxiety is knowing that any choice you make *for* something is also a choice to *miss out* on something else. Without some kind of assurance, the haunting questions within each life choice are these: Did I do the right thing? Was this the best for me, or did I miss the best?

It's so tempting to try to do it all, so as not to miss out. But to do all of those "good things" means you'll do none of them well.

Can You Have It All?

The extraordinary opportunities we have at our fingertips have set up an unfortunate assumption that we all—both women *and* men—need to confront head-on: the belief that we can have it all. Many of us have grown up thinking that we can have it all, but can we really? Is that idea a recipe for empowerment, or will it end in heartbreak and dysfunction?

The truth is, sooner or later everyone discovers that this seductive promise is one that can't be fulfilled. In some ways we may be able to "have it all" over the course of our lifetime—but not all at the same time. For women this most often hits home in the sensitive subject of children and career. Can we have both? Of course. Can anyone simultaneously manage the intense needs of children well and the needs of an intense career? That depends on a host of factors—the use of wisdom, an honest accounting of personal limitations, and family dynamics being chief among them. But regardless, the hard truth is that we can't have it all in the absolute sense. We can't have it all—all at the same time. Something or someone *always* gets left out or deeply hurt when we try.

I (Shaunti) was recently at a women's leadership breakfast where a panel of four female executives were discussing corporate responsibility. One of the panel members was the head of government relations for a Fortune 500 company. As she was speaking, I was struck by her confidence and poise. However, her façade changed when someone asked: "Is there a parallel between corporate responsibility and family responsibility? How do you make sure you give your family the time, attention, and focus they deserve?" This fast-track executive who seemed to have it all together honestly answered, "I don't know how to handle it."

She explained that she was in her mid-thirties and had an eleven-month-old baby. She travels extensively for her job, and her husband also works full-time. Each time she heads home from an international trip, she's not sure how much "awake time" she'll be able to spend with her husband and child before she has to leave again.

It was obvious that this situation was weighing her down when she made herself completely vulnerable by sighing and ending her comments with, "If any of you have learned anything along the way or have any thoughts or advice you wanted to share in that area, I'd sure love to hear it." You won't be surprised to hear that I made a beeline for this woman when the breakfast was over. I explained who I was and that I was working on a video series for women that addressed the very issue she was facing. I told her, "Honestly, I think we women have bought into a myth that we can have it all, all at the same time. But the reality is, if you try to have it all, someone is going to suffer. In your case, it might be your husband or your child. It might be you. Or it might be your colleagues or the projects you're working on. *Something's* going to get hurt. And when we try to do everything, sometimes *everything* gets hurt. We don't talk about this today, but it is so critical not to let life just pick us up and carry us along. We need to be purposeful about making decisions that will help us take control of our lives . . . and our *family's* lives."

She explained that while she knew she couldn't keep up the pace she was going, she didn't have the desire to quit her job entirely and be a stay-at-home mom. But she feared that her new family obligations would start to take their toll on her job performance. And then she told me several stories of ways her boss had already been irritated because she couldn't stay longer on an international trip, while her husband was stressed because he was setting aside his own work projects to be with the baby while she was out of town. She said she realized the clock counting down her days in her current high-travel job would probably start ticking at some point.

I smiled ruefully and said, "Honestly . . . it sounds like the clock is *already* ticking. I'm sure they love you and they would never want to let you go, but the tension is already there. I'm sure you yourself have seen these examples before, where someone who is torn between work and family starts having unhappy people on both ends." She agreed and acknowledged that when she had seen that slide begin, it was always just a matter of time before the person's boss decided that someone else would be able to be more focused on the job, would be able to travel more, and wouldn't be torn between work and home, at which point the person would be either let go or moved into another position.

The trouble was, she sighed, that she didn't want another position. The trouble was, she wanted the globe-trotting position, *and* she wanted a healthy, happy family life. The trouble was, she realized, as we talked, that she wanted it all . . . all at the same time.

I asked her, "If you had to choose, which is your top priority?" She said there was really no question: although she wanted her current job, she didn't want it to be at the expense of damaging her marriage or her child.

Given that reality, my advice to her was to be purposeful right now instead of letting that painful slide happen: that her boss would likely be relieved and respectful if she talked to him in a direct and professional manner about the situation before he had to have "a talk" with her. Since she loved her job, I suggested she design and propose a role for herself that would give her the satisfaction of using her most in-demand skills while also carving out the time and flexibility she needed to be the wife and mother she most wanted to be. Her response stunned me. Soberly, she nodded and said, "It probably is a good idea to be purposeful about it. You're right. I never thought about it that way before." I walked away bemused that this framework is so far from our radar screen that an incredibly smart, experienced woman had never even thought about it before.

Maria Shriver, a celebrated TV commentator and the wife of California Governor Arnold Schwarzenegger, has also learned the hard truth of not being able to have it all. In her book *Ten Things I Wish I'd Known—Before I Went Out into the Real World*, she offers the following advice: "You can't have an exciting, successful, powerful career and at the same time win the mother-of-the-year award and be wife and lover extraordinaire. No one can. If you see successful, glamorous women on magazine covers proclaiming they do it all, believe me, you're not getting the whole story." She then admitted, "Once you have children, you not only can't do it all, you can't do it the same way you were doing it before. In other words, once you start a family, don't expect to be the same hard-driving, workaholic, do-anything, go-anywhere worker you were. Because if you are, your children will suffer."[24]

Our question is: Who else is teaching women that they *can't* have it all? The truth is, not many people are. Most women only discover it's all a myth after they have tried . . . and failed.

The Choice of Childlessness

Of course, this difficult balancing act between family and career can be escaped by simply eliminating children from the equation altogether— or deciding to delay children many years until a career is well-established. Young women are increasingly choosing this option as they see female icons like Oprah and Rachael Ray lead by example. In an interview with *Good Housekeeping* magazine, Ray, the megastar of Food Network, admitted that the demands on her time meant that motherhood would not likely find a spot on her calendar anytime soon. Said Ray, "Now I'm in my late thirties, and I've committed to so much work in the next three years that I think it would be really selfish to attempt to have a child."[25]

Many women today might agree with that sentiment. But think about it for a moment. Is it really selfish to have a child? Or perhaps . . . could there be a selfish reason behind deciding *not* to have one? While the percentage is still small, the number of women ages fifteen to forty-four who say they intend to forego motherhood is the highest its ever been. Most often it's a lifestyle decision. A growing number of couples now rate the value of their work, recreation, and standard of living above that of having children. Anne Hare is one example. According to an AP reporter who interviewed the fitness program coordinator from Georgia, "Hare and her husband made a momentous decision three years ago: They would not have children. It's not that they don't like kids, she says. They simply don't want to alter the lifestyle they enjoy."[26]

A recent *Wall Street Journal* article begins with the following proclamation, "Former General Electric Company Chief Executive Jack Welch has some blunt words for women climbing the corporate ladder: you may have to choose between taking time off to raise children and reaching the corner office." Welch says, "There's no such thing as work-life balance. There are work-life choices, and you make them, and they have consequences."[27] The article goes on to quote some women who agree with Welch and others who don't. His comments sparked a firestorm of debate about the issue.

Now, are there some women who have managed both to lead a company and to raise a family well? Yes, of course. But the fact remains that it is often difficult to balance the two, and that is one of the main reasons for the stark lack of women in the highest levels of business in corporate America.

In fact, when I was interviewing several highly accomplished, godly Christian women in business to get their workplace insight for the expanded (Christian) edition of *The Male Factor*, I suddenly realized something. Of the twelve women I had interviewed, *ten of them did not have children*—primarily due to infertility or a late marriage. There was a *reason* these particular women had risen so high in business: they had the margin in their lives to devote much more time to their careers.

Some women (and men) see that truth and think, *Well I won't have children*. But before heading down the road of *deliberate* childlessness, women and men alike would do well to heed the words of researcher and author Sylvia Ann Hewlett. When she set out to interview scores of highly successful women who were well into their careers, she assumed she would hear stories of celebrity status, power, and money that made children an easy trade-off. But "this is *not* what these women said. Rather, they told haunting stories of children being crowded out of their lives by high-maintenance careers and needy partners. . . . I was taken aback by what I heard. Going into these interviews, I had assumed that if these accomplished, powerful women were childless, surely they had chosen to be. I was absolutely prepared to understand that the exhilaration and challenge of a megawatt career made it easy to decide not to be a mother. Nothing could be further from the truth. When I talked to these women about children, their sense of loss was palpable. I could see it in their faces, hear it in their voices, and sense it in their words."[28]

So basically, some of America's most successful businesswomen confess that even the thrill of climbing to the top doesn't make up for the hole they feel when they set aside one of the ways God has designed them. When you stop and think about it, this is not surprising given that God describes children as one major source of blessing to us; according to Psalm 127, our children are literally like an "inheritance" passed down from our heavenly Father.

And that sense of regret for something missed is not only triggered by choices about children. In a multiopportunity but imperfect world, *anyone*—whether a stay-at-home mom or fast-track executive—can be well-intentioned and still end up making choices that lead to regret instead of the abundant life God intends for her.

A Way to Make the Right Decisions

So here's our question for you. In something like the scenario described by Sylvia Ann Hewlett above, do you think it would have made a difference if those high-powered women had *known in advance* that certain choices would lead to regret instead of delight? Or let's make the question more personal: think about an area of life in which *you* have regret. Would it have made a difference if you could have seen that certain choices would lead you there? We think so.

The problem is that it will take much more than an occasional confessional from a regretful woman to steer us in the right direction. As illustrated by news anchor Alison Stewart, younger women can look at the deep regrets shared by some older career women and still not know what to do about it! Stewart said, "When my friends and I talk about older women . . . part of the conversation always is, 'Gosh, those women have had to give up so much to make those things happen. Should we give up those things?'" That's a good question and is implicitly answered by what Stewart sees in these older women. "I see so many women in their forties and fifties who are struggling with [the question:] did they make the right decisions about their career."[29]

"Did I make the right decisions?" Or, *"What decision should I make?"* Every woman has felt the heart cry of those questions. And every one of us wants the peace of knowing that we *have* made the right decisions for our lives, whether in the big life-changing crossroads (getting married, taking a particular career path, having children . . .) or the little day-to-day choices (accepting a volunteer project, signing the kids up for soccer, or turning down another date with the guy you met recently). Because we all know that in many cases the small decisions can just as easily lead to life-changing impact as the big ones. And no one wants to end up with regret.

Yet to truly change lives (and the culture), we have to go beyond a vague desire to avoid regret. We need a concrete, biblical way to help others and ourselves make the right decisions. That is what the rest of this book is about. And frankly, we need a multitude of wise, godly mentors to reach out to the confused, torn, stressed women of today with a life-giving, clear, biblical way to navigate our world of choices.

> We need a concrete, biblical way to help others and ourselves make the right decisions. That is what the rest of this book is about. ❧

We believe younger women would love for older, life-smart women to step forward and courageously speak into the confusion and empty rhetoric of much of today's modern femininity and offer rock-solid ways to build a life. Young women yearn for the life coaches mentioned earlier—women who can point them to a life that is not only sensible and satisfying (Titus 2:5) but also one that can go the distance without pulling up somewhere lame with regret. Young women—I would argue *all* women—long not just for a godly mentor and friend but also for the sense that this guide can exemplify or cast a biblical vision of hope and direction. A guide who can point that woman to God's best for her life.

You may ask, is there really any way to use Scripture so individually and specifically to guide a twenty-first-century woman? Is there a guide in Scripture that can apply to *all* women and yet not be guilty of cookie-cutter sameness that presses everyone into a common mold? One that will stay fresh even as you grow older? One that can truly guide you to God's best for your life? The answer is yes.

2

A Satisfied Life

So how do we find the best in life? Abraham found it. Consider the words that conclude his life: "Abraham breathed his last and died, . . . an old man and satisfied with life" (Gen. 25:8).

What a way to go! This capstone statement reveals a life rewarded with a deep sense of personal fulfillment and gratification. It also suggests a life with few regrets. In short, life worked for Abraham. It came together with a wow rather than a whimper and paid rich dividends. Is there a woman or man alive today who wouldn't want a life like this? But the question is, what's the secret to living such a satisfied life?

Millions today, probably most of us, look to many different things for satisfaction. It is easy, for example, to consider life good and satisfying if we have a happy marriage, rewarding kids, or a fulfilling job. Some people, of course, look to unhealthier things. It is a particular temptation in America today to look to money to somehow "buy" happiness. The truth is, of course, that it often buys the opposite, especially when it becomes the goal of life. Even scientists agree. Dr. Edward Diener has studied money and its relation to happiness in great detail. He summarized his scientific findings in one short sentence: "Materialism is toxic for happiness."[1]

We would argue that, frankly, *anything* we rely on for happiness or contentment other than God is going to be toxic for happiness in the end. So if love of money, for example, is toxic for happiness, what's the tonic?

The big-picture answer is a relationship with God that is so vibrant we don't rely or lean on anything *but* Him. But the specific *way* that God, through that relationship, leads His people to a satisfying life is this: *purpose*.

Even the medical field has found as much. Dr. William Sheldon of Columbia University Medical School reported, "Continued observations in clinical practice lead almost inevitably to the conclusion that deeper and more fundamental than sexuality, deeper than the craving for social power, deeper even than the desire for possessions, there is a still more generalized and universal craving in the human makeup. It is the craving for knowledge of *right direction*—for orientation."[2] God has a purpose for every person, and deep down, we all long to find it.

We have already established that there are many directions in which we can head. So how do we know which way is the right way? How do we find our purpose? For us, we know studying and searching the Bible are huge assets in this undertaking because it contains a treasure trove of proven guidelines.

Yet many of us already *are* trying to live a godly life and follow the Bible's specific precepts, and we *still* aren't sure exactly which choices to make among all our opportunities and demands on our time. We are still stressed and torn. Many of us might doubt whether, in fact, the Bible can even provide that sort of ultrapractical, day-to-day direction for us as modern women, since the choices that are open to us today couldn't have even been imagined thousands of years ago when the Bible was written.

Yet although our world has changed around us, certain things haven't changed. Our design as human beings hasn't changed from two thousand years ago until today. Our design as women hasn't changed. And the fact that God has given us both universal and individual gifts and callings for His purposes hasn't changed. Just like two thousand years ago, today we can either live in concert with that design and those callings—or in tension with them.

> Although our world has changed around us, our design and callings haven't changed. ॐ

As noted in the introduction, to the degree that our choices are at odds with how we are designed and called, we will experience regret instead of contentment. But as we instead courageously live according to God's blueprint for our lives, we will thrive. And thankfully, one of the great benefits of our "era of opportunity" is that once we have that vision and that *way* to make the right decisions on those opportunities, the stage is set for us as women to make an eternal difference in this world!

No matter what your life looks like, God has a calling and a place that He has specially designed for you. And He *wants* each of us to find it; He doesn't want us to feel overwhelmed, confused, or unclear. But to get that clarity and find God's best for us, we need a guide.

An Unchanging Guide

We can rightly look to the Bible to guide us through life, but we need help to understand how to apply the Bible to the life we live today, since the world we live in looks very different than it did two thousand and four thousand years ago, when the Bible was written.

For centuries, people have recognized that the Bible is filled with timeless wisdom. But the Bible itself says it is not just a book of wisdom; it is God's supernatural revelation. Second Timothy 3:16–17 says, "All Scripture is inspired by God and profitable for teaching, for reproof, for correction, for training in righteousness; so that the man [and woman!] of God may be adequate, equipped for every good work."*

Some of you may be comfortable with the idea that the Bible is the direct words of God to us, but for some of you that may be a new thought. But if the Bible *is* the divine authority it says it is, then we can't just pick and choose which parts we will believe and follow. Either it is all God given and true—and thus should indeed be used as our absolute guide—or it is partly or entirely a collection of man-made writing, in which case we can't depend on any of it to be true.

---

*In this Scripture, the Greek word *anthrōpos*, used here poetically as *man* actually means "mankind" or "human being."

We believe the Bible is what it says it is: authoritative and therefore true in its entirety. So in this book we will be accepting the Bible as our unchanging, authoritative guide. It is important to recognize that if you aren't used to the idea of biblical authority, your reaction to some of the ideas in this book may be more of a reaction to the concept of the authority of the Bible than a reaction to the subject matter itself.

Let me take a moment to illustrate the concept of a reference point that never changes and how that applies to our need for direction. My husband, Jeff, and I started our married life in New York City. All New Yorkers know that there are times when finding direction is difficult because when you come up out of the subway everything looks the same. If you are not familiar with that particular block, you have no idea which direction is which. The city is a giant grid, so it should be easy, but there are skyscrapers all around, and you wonder, *Which direction am I pointing? I'm at 32nd and Madison and need to walk west to get to Times Square, but which way is west?*

Like everyone else in the city, I quickly learned that when I came up above ground and got confused, all I had to do was stop and turn in a circle until I saw the twin towers of the World Trade Center. They were so huge they towered over all the other massive buildings and could always be seen in the distance, at the southern tip of Manhattan.

So when I saw those imposing towers, I knew that direction was south, and then I could figure out all the other directions. If I got turned around again, I just looked up. As with most other New Yorkers, the Twin Towers were my orienting point, and I built my sense of direction on them because they were permanent and unchanging. Until one Tuesday in September 2001, when they came crashing down.

I eventually moved to Atlanta, but when I go back to New York City, it is very disorienting. I don't know where to look to figure out where I am going. Why? I had built a habit of relying for direction on something that one day would crumble. And I was lost without it.

That's the way a lot of us live. Without realizing it, we look to temporary things to orient ourselves, make decisions, and guide us to that abundant life we want. For instance, we might look to our level of happiness in a marriage, career, or activities. We might look to our stress level. We might look to how we're doing on the job, what sort of new opportunities we are offered, or whether or not our kids are behaving. If we're happy, or the job or kids are going well, we check the box in our mind that says, "Life is good; I am not stressed; I am going in the right direction." And based on that, we might say something like, "Sure, I can take on that school mentoring project!" On the other hand, if those factors are challenging we think, *Hm, maybe I need a change of direction* or we say (maybe), "I'm so sorry, but my plate is full, you'll need to find someone else."

Hear us on this: None of those factors are *bad*. But they are all temporary. They are going to change as our life situation changes. *We can't look to those things to orient us or steer us in the right direction.* Instead, we need something that will last and be the same forever: God's Word—and specifically what His Word says about His callings and how He has designed us.

God's Word will never change. It will never crumble. When we are unhappy in our marriage and feel a need for a course correction, we can look at what the Bible says and know that it will be a perfect guide forward. When we are getting bad reviews at the office and need a course correction, we can look at an unchanging standard to tell us which course correction matters most. When we have so many opportunities and choices—*good* choices—competing for attention, we can look at something unchanging and trustworthy to help us make that choice.

The problem is that many of us already think we *are* looking to the Bible (or at least we want to), but we don't see anything in there that speaks to our specific situations today as modern women. We don't see a verse that says, "Here is the choice Susan should make when she has to decide whether to stay in this job or move to another one," or "Ashley should do *this* when her fiancé leaves her at the altar," or "This is what a stay-at-home mom should do when her husband loses his job." What you will discover is that you can find practical guidance in the Bible once you know what to look for. God's unchanging Word is, essentially, a perfect compass that you can trust to get you to God's best for your life.

A Perfect Compass for You

As we go along, we will be finding that this biblical compass will give us direction that is very unique and individual to each of us. And that makes sense because God's design and purpose for *you* will almost certainly be different from His design and purpose for every other woman.

I really enjoyed the first *Pirates of the Caribbean* movie and see in it a great analogy for us. In the movie Captain Jack Sparrow is rather obsessed with his peculiar compass, a compass that doesn't point north. Instead, it points to just one place, the place where his special treasure is buried. With great glee Captain Jack navigates his ship solely based on his individual compass. Picking his way through dense fog and graveyards of wrecked ships, he knows if he relies solely on his individual compass, he will find his treasure.

> You will understand how God's Word creates an individual compass for you to get to God's best—and the action steps to get you there. ☙

This book is designed to help each of us use the Bible to do just that. As you read, you will begin to understand how God's Word creates an individual compass for you to get to God's best, and you will discover clear action steps you need to take to get there. Then, of course, you will have to *decide* to follow God's compass regardless of what you may feel in the fog and regardless of any roadblocks that come your way.

A Clear, Bold Path Around Roadblocks

We want to be sure to acknowledge, here, that some women reading this may feel that they already have that compass, and they have deep peace that they are already in God's best path for their life, no major course adjustments needed. If you are already that biblical "Life Ready Woman" who is clear about her life, bold in her faith, and able to find God's best, you have a particularly rich ability to speak into the lives of other women, and we hope you do.

But many of us have a few things we need to clarify and do first. For example, before we can figure out where to go, we first have to figure out the reasons why we're not already there. If that is you, understanding the roadblocks already in the way will be key to removing, fixing, or navigating around them.

There could be many individual roadblocks; here are five of the most common.

The Pace of Life

The first roadblock for many of us is simply a pace of life that keeps us running so fast, we never purposefully think about the big picture—much less take proactive steps to course-correct. Like the conflicted globe-trotting new-mom executive I spoke with that day, it's just not on our radar screen. We are too stressed, too overloaded, and just plain tired too much of the time.

But Jesus doesn't want us to be overloaded or stressed, and He *does* have an answer for us. Consider what He says in Matthew 11:28–30: "Come to me, all you who are weary and burdened, and I will give you rest. Take my yoke upon you and learn from me, for I am gentle and humble in heart, and you will find rest for your souls. For my yoke is easy and my burden is light" (NIV).

God does not want us to be weary or burdened. Jesus illustrates this by speaking of a yoke, an apparatus and a system designed to protect and help an animal as it tries to pull a heavy load. In our lives this would be the heavy load of life that we are trying to pull around by ourselves. If we will affirmatively take on the life-management system—the yoke—God has designed for us, we will find the direction and protection we need. Even better, Jesus is implying that it is a double yoke. With a double yoke, a dominant and seasoned animal is usually yoked with a learning animal so the learning one can observe and be guided by the other, more experienced animal.

What Jesus is doing here is holding out His design, His boundaries, and His calling on our lives and saying, "Come hitch yourself to Me, take this life and this *way* of living I have designed for you, let Me lead you, and you will find rest even if you pull a heavy load."

Living Contrary to God's Design

As noted earlier, all too often the reason we are overwhelmed or unclear is that we are trying to live in a way that is completely contrary to what God has planned for our lives. We are carrying a yoke, but it is not the one God has designed for our direction and protection as we walk through life with Him. Essentially we are living life in a way God does not intend us to.

It may sound as if we are talking about making sinful choices, and it is true that willful choices that go against God's principles will eventually catch up with us and will usually make us more stressed. But many of us are honestly trying to follow God's principles, and we are still stressed.

Most of us are simply living contrary to God's design specifications for us and to His callings on our lives, and we don't even realize it. The Bible says God has specifically formed each of us. He knew us all before we were born, and He has created us each in a specific way, for a specific purpose, with specific callings. If we don't live according to those callings, we will feel off track. And if we get really far off track, we might find ourselves, at the end of our lives, looking back not with satisfaction and peace but with regret. But if we live according to those callings, life will just seem right.

> Most of us are simply living contrary to God's design specifications for us and to His callings on our lives, and we don't even realize it. ❧

The next chapter will actually dig into many of the common modern-day reasons *why* we as women might be confused or unclear about our design and callings, and chapter 5 will dive directly into what that design and those callings look like.

Disorientation

The third roadblock is that we are all too often disoriented. How do we know what God's principles are? How do we know what His design for us is? How do we know what His callings are? Even if we are totally open to the authority of the Bible, we may honestly not know what the Bible says that still applies to our lives as modern women today. That is why in this book we'll be spending a lot of time on the antidote to disorientation: the clarity and focus the unchanging reference point of God's Word brings to even the most thorny of the modern questions we have today.

Refusing to Submit to God's Word

Another reason we fail to live to the best life God has for us is that even when we do have the perfect compass of God's Word, we sometimes don't want to submit to it. We want what *we* want for our lives; we want to be in control. Selfishly we think, *I want what I want. No one tells me what to do. In me I trust!* The Bible reveals, however, that if we give in to that mind-set we will end up with heartache and regret instead of the abundant life God intends for us.

A Vague Faith

The final roadblock is that overcoming those other four challenges requires a strong, convicted, practical faith, and many of us have a vague faith instead. Often we don't realize this. We sometimes don't even comprehend that we may be letting the tide of life carry us along or that our faith is shallow and not built on deep, practical convictions from the Bible. For that reason it is important to be purposeful about looking at developing biblical guidance on issues you may have never thought about before. That is why we will develop some firm, practical anchors in this book. You will end up with not only deep biblically based convictions you can refer to for the rest of your life but with firm action steps you can start applying immediately.

To develop these firm, practical convictions, we will be reading and referring to the Bible not just as a set of moral principles that have stood the test of time but as a living guide straight from God that applies directly to us individually. In part 2 of this book, you will find five specific Faith Steps drawn from the Bible that will require moving from vague faith to active faith.

These Faith Steps are not hard to understand, but they require boldness and courage. More importantly, they will lead you to God's best for your life. They have worked this way in many women's lives, and they will work in yours as well. We will begin unpacking the first of these Faith Steps in chapter 6. But first let's look at the major issues women are struggling with today—issues these Faith Steps are meant to resolve.

3

What the Issues Actually Are

A good counselor has the ability to distinguish between issues and problems. That's a gift of insight many people don't have; to most of us, issues and problems look and feel the same. But they're not—in fact, they are as different as cause and effect. Our problems are really just a visible display of deeper, less apparent, unresolved issues that must be rooted out and dealt with.

For example, think of someone you know who has trouble relating to a family member. They fight. They don't get along. They can't communicate. Those are very real and serious problems. But the real *issue* behind that struggle may actually be a secret jealousy or a need to control other people.

As a pastor, I (Robert) have seen people deal all their lives with one difficulty after another but never identify or address the issue that's actually fueling their problems. It's easy to have this blind spot. I know because I've fallen prey to it firsthand. I once brought in a highly regarded consultant to help me with a number of serious problems I was having in leading our church. For several hours I poured out to him my frustrations with staff, organization, time demands, directional challenges, and personal concerns. Honestly, I was really hurting. From time to time, the consultant would ask probing questions to aid his understanding of my situation.

Eventually, I finished venting my list of nagging problems. I was eager to hear what ideas he would offer to help solve all of them. Pen in hand, I prepared to take notes.

After a long pause he looked at me and said, "Robert, you're tired." I quickly acknowledged that but waited for him to get down to real answers for solving my predicament.

But that *was* his answer.

With laser-like insight, he had named the issue behind all my troubles. And as the day went on, he helped me see that most of my current undoing was either exaggerated or self-inflicted because of exhaustion. The reason I was so overwhelmed and confused was simply because I was out of gas. "Fatigue makes cowards of us all," he said. "What you need is some time off to recharge your batteries and put life back into perspective."

At that moment time off was the last thing I thought I needed. But his advice proved to be on target. And by heeding his wise counsel and addressing the root issue—not working harder or smarter on the problems resulting from it—I found the real help I needed to get my life back together.

So what does that mean for you? How can you determine the issues behind your problems? First you need to identify your problems. Take a look at the detailed list of struggles on page 37 that women say they face in the twenty-first century. Grab a pen and circle the hot phrases you can personally identify with—or add others.

Now keep those problems in mind as you continue reading. Many of them likely spring from deeper issues that often remain hidden and unresolved.

Let's use a word picture to demonstrate this. Imagine your life as a valley fed and crisscrossed by mountain springs. God intends your "valley" to be green, fertile, peaceful, and abundant. Instead, it is brown in some places. Sure, there are beautiful areas of green grass and abundant fruit, but there are also areas marred by surprising blight. In one spot crops stubbornly won't grow; in another, grass dies. In yet another the pools have turned to smelly marshes.

Those visible problems could all be "coincidental" and have nothing to do with one another, or they could be signs that something is poisoning or

PROBLEMS WOMEN SAY THEY STRUGGLE WITH

Circle all that apply and add others.

- time management
- accomplishing goals
- making financial decisions
- taking care of everyone (even adult kids)
- figuring out what I should do
- parenting my children God's way
- security
- trying to fill all roles well
- balancing attention between children and husband
- redefining my life after divorce
- being allowed to be the biblical woman I want to be
- not enough time and energy to do all I want to do
- not knowing where I fit in
- being everything to everyone
- parenting teenagers
- direction and purpose
- feeling worthwhile as a homemaker
- organizing/prioritizing
- meeting my own expectations
- expectations of others
- not being so assertive
- maintaining focus
- time vs. money
- not doing enough
- what to do with the rest of my life
- living with a difficult, angry man
- being average
- balancing motherhood, career, and marriage
- being left alone
- missing out on my kids growing up
- failure as a mother and woman of God
- not having left a legacy for someone
- loneliness, isolation
- growing old
- not reaching my potential
- not having skills to support myself if I suddenly had to (and not wanting to)
- financial security, retirement
- a bad relationship with a man
- making sure I'm all that I can be
- wondering where my marriage is going
- being a good mother and wife
- intimacy
- really trusting God
- finding a godly man who is not intimidated by me
- being 36 and single
- relationships
- feeling inadequate
- making it
- failure
- raising my sons without a father presence or role model
- working full-time
- proving myself
- learning who God wants me to become
- handling power struggles at work
- my job
- saying no
- contentment in finances
- marriage that gets harder as years go by (25 years)
- single mom trying to be everything
- guilt
- abusive marriage
- thinking outside myself and my needs
- questioning if I'm a godly wife and mother
- my identity, discovering who I am
- what to give my life to
- choosing the best
- staying faithful
- not understanding men
- thrown into working world after divorce
- finding boundaries of independence/freedom
- trusting my husband's choices
- really loving my husband

fouling the water upstream. Rather than treating the fruit trees, the grass, and the marshes separately, wouldn't it make more sense to follow the springs upstream? So you trace the streams to their source, find the toxins and eliminate them, and clear, life-giving water brings life to the valley, which blooms unspoiled again.

Similarly, identifying and resolving the issues "upstream" that cause our problems can be life changing. When issues remain open and unresolved, they lead not only to those problems but to confusion and bad decision-making. But when these issues are identified, understood, and addressed with biblical convictions, many of the problems flowing from them naturally work themselves out or can be successfully dealt with.

What the Issues Are

So what are the most common issues behind many of the problems in the lives of women today? There are five. And each issue causes problems *because it leads us to live contrary to how we are designed.* So let's take a look at these issues that make it so easy to do that—those elements that poison or confuse the groundwater. (And keep your pen handy to circle any issues that could be contributing to the problems you circled on page 37.)

Issue 1: An Ever-Evolving Femininity

What does it mean to be a woman today? There is no commonly accepted answer and certainly not one with biblical roots. Even the images the word *woman* brings to mind have changed significantly over the last generation. Fifty years ago when people heard this word, they were more than likely to associate it with words like *soft, sensitive, submissive, nurturing, pretty,* and *virtuous.* But times have changed. Now words like *assertive, strong, confident, sexy, independent,* and *equal* are typically used to describe the modern woman.

Our culture has also added new ideas of what it means *to be* a woman. Hillary Clinton set the tone for the new woman when she quipped on her husband's 1992 campaign trail that she was not about "to stay home and bake cookies" and "be some little woman standing by her man."

Actress Sharon Stone went even further. I (Robert) can still remember being stunned years ago when I read this quote from the actress: "As I see it, the choice today is between being feminine and equal. I choose equal."[1] Although most women today, thankfully, have come to realize that we don't have to choose between the two, it is indisputable that everywhere we look new voices continue to redefine and reshape what it means to be a woman.

Christians cannot help but be influenced by the sweeping sociological changes we encounter nearly every day, even if we don't realize we are being influenced. In our postmodern world it's easy to think of being a woman as nothing more than a cultural construct that we can live out based on personal choice. But for women of faith, personal choice should first yield to deeper questions, such as: How does God define me as a woman? Is there a basic biblical pattern for womanhood that might supersede and direct my personal preferences and choices? The Scriptures offer life-defining answers to these questions, which will be discussed in detail in the next few chapters.

For now, let's look at the significant status changes that have marked the lives of women since the 1950s. They have been as dramatic as the changes in women's hairstyles. Just as salons during the past sixty years have followed the trend from the beehive to Charlie's Angels to "the Rachel" and beyond, a woman's social identity has also shifted from one role paradigm to another, as illustrated and then described below.

The Swinging Social Pendulum

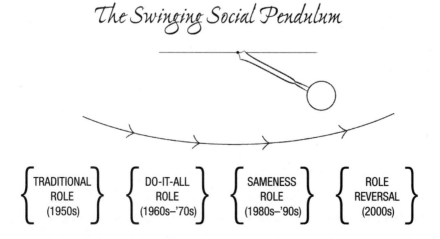

| { TRADITIONAL ROLE (1950s) } | { DO-IT-ALL ROLE (1960s–'70s) } | { SAMENESS ROLE (1980s–'90s) } | { ROLE REVERSAL (2000s) } |

THE TRADITIONAL ROLE

Characterized by the sitcoms of the 1950s, this was an era of Ozzie and Harriet, strict social decorum, well-defined and separated gender patterns, and patriarchal authority. Young girls played with dolls, put on practice teas, and paid close attention to etiquette. They typically did well in school, but often their primary aim was to marry and have a family. Women who desired to pursue careers outside the home were rare as were women who cohabited or remained single.

"A woman's place is in the home" was the slogan that carried the day. That not only meant that a woman supposedly best served society by getting married and staying home with her children, but it also strongly implied that a woman should leave the broader world of professional ambitions to men. Many churches endorsed this stereotype as *the* biblical model of womanhood despite biblical examples to the contrary (Judg. 4:4; Prov. 31:16; Acts 16:14; 18:1–3, 26).

THE DO-IT-ALL ROLE

Social traditions were shattered in the radical '60s and the psychedelic '70s. In this era almost everything for a woman came into question: her role, her place, her value, her virginity, and even the sacred ground of marriage. Why not merely live together? It was a wild time of free love for many women and men, and some unfortunately paid for it later. But at this moment freedom from traditional restraints was intoxicating.

Married women were liberated too. They were told they could have it all, especially when it came to work and home. "If I have to, I can do anything. I am strong, I am invincible, I am woman," proclaimed Helen Reddy in her hit song. From this age of idealism, the concept of the super-mom was born. This idea, however, was short-lived. By the end of the '70s, many working moms were tasting the bitterness of reality and exhaustion that comes with trying to do it all.

One such mom confessed to Oprah Winfrey, "I tried hard to be the supermom, but frankly I wasn't good at it. Looking back, it was costly. I had a very angry little girl who wanted her mommy, and I didn't have the time, and I didn't know how to balance it. It took me a long time to understand that you can't have it all."[2] But there was no going back to the '50s. A new womanhood had been uncorked, and if supermom wasn't the answer, then something else was.

THE SAMENESS ROLE

In the '80s and '90s a new form of femininity arose, one that was more realistic but also more aggressive and assertive. Women would no longer try to do it all. Instead, they began to expect men to share every facet of life with them fifty-fifty. Which sounds fine at first, but in practice it meant many women wanted to do away with all gender distinctions at home, work, and play. Columbia University's Carolyn Heilbrun argued for this idea in her book *Reinventing Womanhood*. A husband's career should never take priority over his wife's, and his care-giving duties at home should match hers exactly, said Heilbrun. She justified her "symmetrical family" model on the claim that gender differences are the result of society, not a creation of divine design. Heilbrun believes that a mother's tenderness reflects the manipulative forces of social persuasion, not her nature. And if men are less motherly, it's the culture, not nature, that's to blame. The no-roles sameness model was "scientific," said the social critics, and "destined to be the dominant family form of the future."[3]

While all this sounds fair and balanced, the problem is men and women are *not* the same. Equal? Yes, absolutely. But God has created us to be different in many ways. Today science confirms this, and we can see that when God created us "male" and "female" on purpose (Gen. 1:27), those differences mean something good, both practically and theologically.

During this time women also encountered another hard lesson. As they sought to "be like men" in the workplace and vied for promotion and advancement, they learned something men had found earlier: companies want *more*. The concept of sameness may have advanced women's professional lives in some ways, but after hours it quickly became a home breaker. And children were often the ones wounded by it the most.

Just as companies are known for the slippery slope of wanting more, the evolution of women's "sameness" expectations and desires has led to something even further along on the social pendulum: role reversal.

ROLE REVERSAL

A new evolution of woman is arising in these first decades of the twenty-first century. It's a feminine transformation defined by a social realignment occurring more frequently between men and women. And what exactly is that? Simply this: men and women are switching roles. It's the '50s traditional model in reverse.

More and more women are leading the men in their lives—whether in the practical sense of providing for the family or in the relational sense of having the final say. Financially, more and more women are the primary breadwinners for their families. And more men are working less and staying at home with the kids. Look at what has happened in just a few short years. In 2003, there were 5.3 million stay-at-home moms and 98,000 stay-at-home dads.[4] By 2009, the number of stay-at-home moms dropped slightly to 5.1 million, while the number of stay-at-home dads increased *by more than 60 percent,* to 158,000, and that increasing trend shows no signs of stopping.[5] We should note that this is not simply a matter of personal choice: 80 percent of those who lost their jobs during the 2008–2009 recession were men, thrusting many women into the role of sole income earner out of economic necessity.

Relationally the numbers of the "woman in charge" are probably even larger, where a family's pendulum is not settling on husband and wife as equals, but where the wife calls most of the shots.

So where does this swinging socioeconomic pendulum leave women? Often it leaves them confused, stressed, or torn. Because *none* of those societal paradigms are actually biblical—none fit precisely with how we are designed. By contrast, understanding and living by a biblical paradigm will put us right in sync with how God has designed us. It will feel right. An amazing clarity, confidence, and problem-solving ability comes when you can look at a solid, life-giving, biblical road map to guide you through even the broadest social confusion—or the problems that spring from it. We will begin outlining that biblical paradigm in chapter 4.

Issue 2: A New Supreme Pursuit

Life today, especially for young women, has been turned upside down. A radical and profound idea has been introduced and propagated concerning what life is really all about. Young women are bombarded with slogans and images in the media, taught from grade school through the university, and told indirectly by what they see honored among women that a career is the ultimate goal in life.

According to nearly everyone, career success is modern man or woman's supreme pursuit against which all else should be measured. So today, society rarely talks to young men about how to prepare to be a great husband or father. And we guard girls against stereotypes that make motherhood and domestic life seem like a primary (much less divine) calling. Every time we speak to them about aiming high, we're thinking of careers in medicine, law, business, or the like, which is great in isolation, but the cumulative effect of all this is to invite young women to put off, discount, or deny altogether some of their most powerful, God-given drives.

I (Robert) recently attended a high-school homecoming football game. At halftime the announcer introduced the members of the homecoming court. For each of the young ladies, he mentioned their accomplishments and future aspirations. Doctors, lawyers, bankers, teachers . . . the aspirations were high. Wonderful! But I realized they were entirely career-oriented. As I sat in the stands, I began to wonder how the crowd might react if one of the girls had named motherhood and homemaking as her chief ambition. Honestly, it would have sounded odd. Many would consider that option to be a second-rate, backward choice.

Author and teen culture commentator Vicki Courtney agrees with this assessment. In her book *5 Conversations You Must Have with Your Daughter,* she says, "God forbid that any of our girls say they are looking forward to becoming wives and mothers! They will likely be met with pitying stares that imply they lack common sense or the smarts to make it on their own."[6] Lest you think she's overstating the matter, consider the words of former Brandeis professor Linda Hirshman, who spoke for today's culture when she wrote, "Housekeeping and child rearing [are] not worthy of the full-time talents of intelligent and educated human beings."[7] Her book for today's woman is appropriately titled *Get to Work*.

Lucy, a woman in my (Shaunti's) core Life Ready group and the owner of a small business, had the following to say about her challenge in this area, "One of my biggest challenges with living the biblical perspective is my own worldview. When I was growing up my parents didn't tell me that I needed to be a wife and have children and also use my gifts and talents for God's work. They raised me to have a good education and take care of myself. Then if I did meet a husband that was great. But if he became a deadbeat I would have something to fall back on. So my challenge now is how to reconcile that with a biblical perspective."

By definition Lucy's parents implicitly placed career and independence higher on the value scale than family, even if they never would have thought of it that way. We can all too easily fall into the same trap. And our choices will flow from what we implicitly value most.

Now we firmly believe we should encourage many dreams in our daughters or other young women, but we need to help them see the reality of their choices. And we need to help them see that dreams of a godly husband, children, and family life are just as God given as dreams of impact beyond the home. In *5 Conversations*, Vicki Courtney recounts the following interaction:

> *I struck up a conversation with a dear Christian mother whose daughter expressed a dream of someday becoming a physician. Her daughter also looks forward to the day she will marry and have children and wants to be engaged in her husband and children's lives. She had her daughter define* engaged *by asking her more pointed questions. Then this wise mother suggested that they ask female physicians if it is in fact possible to be a doctor and be engaged (as defined by her daughter) in your children's lives. I don't know what her daughter will ultimately decide to do, but I do know she is reevaluating her dream based on the answers she is gathering. Imagine if more mothers were helping their daughters do this sort of due diligence before they sink*

large sums of money and time into a career path that may leave them
disillusioned in the end.[8]

Again, it is not that dreams for a particular career path are wrong! But it is vital for us to be completely aware of what results might flow from our choices, and address any issues that need to be addressed, so that we don't find ourselves with deep, unintended regrets. What we decide—what *you* decide—depends on how some deeply philosophical questions are answered: What should be the supreme pursuit of my life? Around what should everything else in my life be ordered? How can I best steward my divine callings and gifts from an eternal perspective? All of those questions will be addressed in later chapters.

Issue 3: Successfully Engaging a Man

If engaging a man feels as if it has become more difficult, it has! Stephanie Coontz, the author of a comprehensive book on the history of marriage, says, "Relations between men and women have changed more in the past thirty years than they did in the previous three thousand."[9]

Change isn't necessarily a bad thing, especially in any community that viewed women as property of the husband rather than equal in the sight of God. But as we noted earlier, this social revolution threw out some of the good with the bad, redefining certain ideas about how men, women, and marriage are designed—ideas that had often facilitated healthy relationships.

Today, polls indicate the greatest pessimism women have today is about their love lives. Single women keep asking, "Where have all the men gone?" They are frustrated and bewildered at the timidity and passivity of modern men—and with just cause. A recurring complaint is that men no longer take the initiative. They seem to run from it as if from an infectious disease.

On many college campuses "the date" is becoming extinct. *New York Times* columnist David Brooks shares the following personal encounter he recently had with a group of students.

One night over dinner at a northern college, a student from the South mentioned that at her local state university, where some of her friends go, they still have date nights on Friday. The men ask the women out, and they go as couples. The other students at the dinner table were amazed. The only time many young people have ever gone out on a formal date was their high school senior prom. You might as well have told them that in some parts of the country there are knights on horseback jousting with lances.[10]

More and more with men, young women are having to step forward first to make the call, take the lead, and set the pace in a relationship.

Women are also changing the ways they engage men long-term. Casual sex is up; so is living together. So is having a family without a man. In 2007, a record 39.7 percent of births were to unwed mothers.[11] Four in ten! The most dramatic increase is with women in their twenties. "More American women than ever are putting motherhood before matrimony," reported *Newsweek* writers Debra Rosenberg and Pat Wingert.[12]

Unmarried women are today's fastest-growing demographic.[13] When a woman does meet a man she desires to commit to, what are the rules of engagement that will make the relationship last? Does she know? Does he agree? What roles will they play in their new life together? With all of the options out there, how do they know what will work?

So what are the conditions that bring a man and a woman together in happiness? How can women wisely engage with the men in their lives? We'll take a look at this important issue in chapter 9.

Issue 4: The Challenge of Motherhood

What does it take to be a good mother, especially when a career is mixed in? The "mommy wars" pitting working women against home-makers has marked the deep divide that exists over this issue. It's one loaded with hard choices, intense feelings of guilt for problems both real and imagined, personal ambitions, and economic necessities. We will address this issue at length in later chapters.

Being a mother is like being a teacher, nurse, chef, guidance coun-selor, mediator, playmate, policeman, chauffer, and air traffic controller all rolled into one. If stay-at-home moms struggle to fit all this into a single day, mothers who work full-time outside the home face even greater challenges.

In a landmark report fittingly entitled "The Harried Life of the Working Mother," the Pew Foundation analyzed its 2009 survey that found 62 percent of employed moms would love to work part-time if they could (up from 48 percent in 1997). (Separately, a 2000 poll in California found that 62 percent would prefer to work part-time, *from home*.)[14] But financial concerns often rule this out. In 2007, 68 percent of women whose youngest child was between three and five years of age were working outside the home.[15] Working mothers and fathers often struggle with whether they're spending enough "face time" with their children. They know it's important for their kids, and they often have to make difficult choices.

As we have already mentioned, the pressure and the toll of trying to juggle children and career ambitions have become so great that a new trend is developing in America today: young women are choosing to have fewer children or none at all.

The fertility rate in 2007 was 2.1 births per woman.[16] At this rate American parents are barely managing to replace themselves. For increas-ing numbers of women, opting for motherhood is no longer automatic or a top priority.

For Christians, God's callings to "be fruitful and multiply, and fill the earth, and subdue it" in Genesis 1:28 have not gone away. Rightly under-stood (which we will tackle in chapter 5), it is a sacred charge for both men and women to commit to raise and launch a healthy next generation that is able to bless the world with the righteousness of God. For Christians the question should not be simply, Will we choose to embrace this God-given command? but rather, Do we know (or want to face) what our children really need from us to grow up healthy and become godly influencers in the world?

In our demanding, fast-paced, pricey, career-oriented culture, having both the wisdom about God's biblical callings and design and the courage to make hard choices is now an absolute necessity for addressing this crucial issue of parenthood.

Issue 5: The Maze of Unlimited Choices

I (Robert) remember the lively interaction I had with a futurist back in the late 1980s. As a researcher, his job was to assess specific kinds of data that could reveal coming cultural changes. In our discussion I asked him pointedly what he considered to be the most significant change looming before us. I don't know what I expected, but his answer surprised me. "Choices," he said. "The greatest change and challenge in the next generation will be in dealing with the plethora of choices you will have."

His prophecy is now our reality. We have unlimited choices as well as the freedom to pursue them. As we discussed in chapter 1, this is both a blessing and a curse. It's a blessing because now more than ever, women can pursue their dreams. But it can also be a curse because the reality of so many choices demands a new skill that many of us (women and men) lack: the ability to choose rightly.

> "For the first time [people] . . . will have to manage themselves. And society is totally unprepared for it." —Peter Drucker ❧

One of America's greatest management thinkers, the late Peter Drucker, made the following observation shortly before his death in 2006. He wrote, "In a few hundred years, when the history of our time will be written from a long-term perspective, it is likely that the most important event historians will see is not technology, not the Internet, not e-commerce. It is an unprecedented change in the human condition. For the first time—literally—substantial and rapidly growing numbers of people have choices. For the first time, they will have to manage themselves. And society is totally unprepared for it."[17]

Our lives as twenty-first-century citizens are no longer fixed, linear, and one-dimensional. We no longer simply grow up, get married, have children, and die. No, today our lives are wide open, fluid, multidimensional, and besieged by choices and options. Pamela Norris underscored this reality when she wrote, "Women are still trying out different plots at different stages of their lives. There is no definitive path to tread, just multiple possibilities."[18] All of this shouts a huge question: How do you manage these options, choose between them, and not get burned by big regrets?

Navigating the Maze Well from the Start

Everyone needs help when it comes to identifying our issues, "managing ourselves," and navigating this modern maze. Each chapter that follows will help you build your own life-giving biblical compass to guide you through that maze, one that includes ultra-practical solutions individual to your unique life and situation.

And as with any maze, the only way to get through is to turn the right direction from the very beginning. When I (Shaunti) was in college in Colonial Williamsburg, my friends and I often ran through the sculptured greenery maze in the grounds of the Governor's Palace. (Often at night, after the grounds were technically closed, but that's another story . . .) The caretakers updated the route regularly, and upon setting foot in the maze, we always were immediately confronted with the most important choice: turn left or right from the start? If you've ever been in a maze like that at a park or botanical garden, you have experienced the reality that if you turned the wrong way from the beginning, no matter how far you run, you'll never find your way out. You'll need to go all the way back to the beginning and start off in the correct direction.

In our lives, starting with a biblical understanding of womanhood, marriage, and family, is just like that. We need to know how we fit into God's system for humanity and human relationships in order to make the right choice on our new Life Ready path from the beginning. We will cover those subjects in chapter 4.

4

A Biblical Definition of Womanhood, Marriage, and Family

*I*t would be pretty confusing to try to understand all the steps discussed in the rest of this book without first having a good biblical understanding of (1) what it means to be a man or a woman, (2) what the Bible says about marriage, and (3) what it looks like to have a biblical family. Without this biblical paradigm or framework, there is simply no way for us to live fully the life God has planned for us because by definition we could be trying to operate at odds with how we are designed and not realize it.

Before we dive into these three subjects, including some that can be controversial in our culture, let us repeat one crucial point. As we said in chapter 2, we are approaching this whole book from a position of faith that the Bible is what it says it is—God's authoritative Word to us—and thus that we should pattern our lives after its model. We recognize that some readers may not share this worldview. If you are in that category (and perhaps even if you aren't), you may find at least some of the conclusions in this chapter surprising or even hard to swallow.

We have no desire to force a particular pattern of living on anyone. And we certainly do not judge anyone with other views. We do, however, unapologetically believe that in the Bible our Creator does clearly lay out certain personal, marriage, and family patterns He has created us for and asks us to follow and that following these patterns (even if they seem counterintuitive at first!) will lead to the abundant life, joy, and peace He promises, instead of stress, heartache, and regret. While there is no way we as human beings could ever present or follow God's ways perfectly or even understand them fully, what we describe below is our best effort at capturing the biblical model.

The Wonderful Differences between Us

There is a distinct and clear difference in how men and women are designed. Every branch of science from neuroscience to anthropology now confirms something that the Bible has laid out all along. Of course, we believe that those differences are good and there for a reason: God has an intended framework for what a man should be and what a woman should be. And every part of our identities will be affected by how we live out that design.

Most of us today would agree that yes, men and women are different, and move on. But without a clear biblical definition of manhood and womanhood, without a clear vision of *how* they are different and *why*, both men and women have trouble separating life-giving pursuits from mistakes and mirages. There is nothing specific to aspire to, strive for, or check ourselves against. "Am I a good woman?" "Did I behave like a man today?" If God really has created us male and female for a purpose, those are absolutely essential questions. And the only place the life-giving, encouraging answers can be found is in a biblical understanding of maleness and femaleness.

We learn in Genesis that of all the things God created, none is more meaningful than humanity. Men and women stand as equals at the apex of God's created order. In Genesis 1:27 we read, "God created man in His own image, in the image of God He created him; male and female He created them." Here we learn that women and men were designed to reflect God's image over the rest of creation. But just as important is what lies at the heart of this design. Of all things it is gender: male and female.

The thing we must first decide is whether we're going to believe this central tenet. This is a crucial first turn in the maze, the divide for living life. *Did* God create us special, and is one's gender purposeful, or are we all merely a product of random chance? Our decision here has huge ramifications for how we proceed in life and view masculinity and femininity. Of course, you can choose to believe that everything exists by pure accident and that nothing has a fixed purpose. If that's the case, then you are left to create your own definition of manhood and womanhood. On the other hand, if God created the universe as Genesis says He did and you believe it, then you find yourself called to embrace a breathtaking dignity and fixed meaning to your life and to your womanhood. You are purposeful, designed, intentional, and God has put you here because He is out to achieve something in the gender He has wrapped you in. The same is true for men.

We will delve into the specific *callings* that are unique to women in the next chapter, but for now let's take a look at what makes a man a man and what makes a woman a woman.

Biblical Manhood

How does the Bible define a man, a *real* man? We find that a vision of manhood is inspired by history's two most influential men. Both are called Adam, the Hebrew word for *man*. Both have left indelible marks on the human race. At times Scripture plays them up as opposites—two men who made radically different choices and pursued equally different lifestyles. But when they are brought together *as men*, they provide us with a way to envision and define biblical manhood.

The first of these two Adams is the Adam of Genesis. He was divinely fitted for masculine success. Strong, intelligent, favored by God—the whole earth was his to rule and subdue. He was set for a great adventure. All he had to do was get three things right.

1. Adam had a *will* to obey.
2. Adam had *work* to do.
3. Adam had a *woman* to love and care for.

These were Adam's responsibilities as a man. But we know from Genesis 3 that Adam failed on each of these counts in one fell swoop.

Standing under the boughs of a forbidden tree, he refused to obey God's will and he "checked out" instead of doing the hard work of manly leadership; in utter selfishness he refused to protect his wife from the serpent's seductive advances and then blamed her. His mistakes come down to one simple theme: he lost his masculine focus, and without it he became passive. Sadly, this passive masculinity is part of the sin that has been passed down through the ages.

Generations later we find a second Adam, literally "the second man"—Jesus. The Gospels make clear that Jesus is God the Son, the Creator of the universe, and humanity's only hope for salvation. But they also make sure we know Jesus was *a man*: flesh and blood, mind and heart—like every other man who ever lived. And as history's second Adam, Jesus unveiled a new vision of masculinity even as His life paralleled the life of the first Adam with the same three responsibilities.

1. Jesus had a *will* to obey.
2. Jesus had a *work* to do.
3. Jesus had a *woman* to love and care for.

Like Adam, Jesus the man was obligated to submit to the will and work of God. He also had a woman to love. Scripture calls her the bride of Christ. She is the church—every Christian throughout the generations. So how did Jesus' new masculinity supersede Adam's failed one?

As with Adam, Jesus' greatest test took place in a garden. Would He allow Himself to be betrayed, captured, beaten, crucified, and separated from the Father to pay the price for the sins of everyone else? Or would he slip away into the darkness and protect Himself, as the human part of His nature was screaming at Him to do? It was *the* moment for both His life and His masculinity. All of His God-given responsibilities came together during a night of grief and betrayal. Set before Him was God's way, and, of course, the other option we all have . . . *my* way. Jesus' understanding of His humanity and masculinity called Him to submit to His Father's will even though it would cost Him unspeakable agony and death. Adam's example, on the other hand, offered Him another option: choose selfishness and passivity over responsibility.

You know how the story ends. To paraphrase Romans 5:15, through one man (Adam) the world cascaded into death, but through a second man (Jesus), the way of salvation and new life was opened to all. So while Adam failed his manhood test in the Garden of Eden, Jesus triumphed with His in the Garden of Gethsemane. "Not as I will, but as You will," He cried (Matt. 26:39). Rejecting passivity, He selflessly loved His bride and bravely took a stand for His responsibilities even though it cost Him everything. Jesus obeyed the Father's call because He trusted the Father's promise that the suffering of the cross was a necessary part of the journey to greater glory. "For the joy set before Him," Jesus endured the cross, Hebrews 12:2 says. In the end Jesus' courageous leadership showed all men what the first man's didn't: God's will, however difficult it may appear or feel at any given moment, ultimately results in a richer, more abundant life and greater reward. This was the vision Jesus held onto in modeling a thoroughly masculine life.

So it's in bringing Adam and Jesus together that we discover true biblical manhood. By noting the parallels between these two towering masculine figures, their points of departure, and the different responses each had to his specific manhood responsibilities, we can create a biblical definition of manhood:

> *A real man rejects passivity, accepts responsibility,*
> *leads courageously, and expects God's greater reward.**

Biblical Womanhood

Does Scripture provide for women a pattern for envisioning biblical womanhood like that provided by comparing Adam and Jesus? If Jesus is the second Adam, can we find any woman presented in the Bible as a sort of second Eve—as a good role model to offset the bad? Yes—Mary.

---

*This vision is at the core of Men's Fraternity, which we highly recommend as a compelling resource for men who want to be equipped in biblical manhood. See *Men's Fraternity: The Quest for Authentic Manhood,* available from LifeWay. You can also preview it at www.mensfraternity.com.

Just as Eve was in the middle of the high drama opening the Old Testament, Mary, a young virgin from Nazareth, stood in the spotlight in the powerful events opening the New Testament. Eve's foolish choices were used to introduce sin and death into the world. Conversely, we can see how Mary's courageous choices played a central role in helping to bring forgiveness and life back to the world.

Mary characterized exemplary virtue and bold, extraordinary faith. She actually *lived* the life the first Eve abandoned. But even more important for our purposes, Mary's life, when contrasted with Eve's, helps us put together a biblical definition of authentic womanhood. Looking at these two women, three significant issues stand out that serve as building blocks for constructing a vision of authentic womanhood.

First, both Mary and Eve were offered the chance to accept or reject God's Word. God had told Adam that no one could eat the fruit of this one tree that would give human beings supernatural knowledge. Yet Eve then listened to the serpent when he questioned what God had said to Adam. And Eve responded by choosing to believe the deceiver rather than embracing God's callings and the goodness she already enjoyed from Him. Mary, however, was a different story. She was confronted with an almost unbelievable situation that—from a worldly perspective—might have seemed to ruin her life. God had made her pregnant before marriage! But He gave her His promise that this pregnancy of bearing the Son of God would make her life special too. It was an awkward, overwhelming situation. After this encounter Mary could have easily panicked and submitted to an abortion (readily available in that era) or to a secret divorce; she could have fled, leaving God's calling far behind. But Mary instead showed remarkable faith. She stood her ground and chose to embrace God's calling on her life. Eve foolishly shunned God's word, but Mary embraced it.

Next we see the actions that flowed from each woman's belief. In Eve's case it can be summarized in two words: she ate (Gen. 3:6). In this one act of willful disobedience, Eve abandoned not only God but also the Core Callings He had set forth to bless her life: to be a partner and helpmate to Adam, to nurture the next generation, and to be a kingdom builder. She abandoned those real, vibrant callings for the alluring mirage of grander things. Conversely, Mary's wise choice of trusting God's Word led to a completely different set of actions. She didn't strike out on her own or seek to end her pregnancy. In fact, she did just the opposite. In spite of the fear she undoubtedly felt at times, she drew closer to God, cherished her pregnancy, carried through with her marriage to Joseph, and courageously embraced God's astounding calling to raise His son!

Finally, we look at each woman's expectations. Both Mary and Eve expected good to come from their beliefs and actions. Eve obviously envisioned even greater personal fulfillments and adventures than God's callings could provide. Her imagination, no doubt, ran wild. *What new freedoms will being like God give me? What wonders will knowing everything, good and evil, open to me? How much greater will I be? How much happier?* It was the life she'd been missing, though before that fateful moment she likely hadn't thought *anything* was missing. But now, caught up in the serpent's words, it all sounded too good to pass up. So Eve went for the life she believed could offer her more than God had given. And indeed she found more—more pain, sorrow, and regret than she knew existed.

Mary expected great reward too, but in her case it circled back to what God had promised her. We admire the courageous obedience she displayed, especially when we know the major payoff was still many hard years away. But Mary's faith held firm to God's Word. Amazingly, she exulted in God's goodness to her before any of the really good results came to pass. In Luke 1:48–49 she said, "For he has been mindful of the humble state of his servant. From now on all generations will call me blessed, for the Mighty One has done great things for me—holy is his name" (NIV).

Mary was celebrating God's goodness at a time when all she could reasonably see was the scandal that would soon visit her. She was about to be a social outcast and a cause for gossip. Yet with the eyes of faith, she trusted God and believed her life would be blessed with His best *in spite of the hardship*. Nine months later that's exactly what she got.

By contrasting these two women's responses to God, to temptation, and to what each considered the better life, we find a biblical definition of authentic womanhood that offers direction to any woman's life:

A biblical woman embraces God's callings, chooses wisely, lives courageously, and expects God's greater reward.

Biblical Marriage

Now that we can see a biblical definition of godly manhood and womanhood, let's take a look at God's design for marriage, a discussion that can help both those currently married and those single but looking ahead. Unlike our biblically generated definitions for manhood and womanhood that we can piece together by contrasting two archetypes, Scripture provides an explicit outline for marriage. It can be awkward to talk about because it is all too often misunderstood, and in a moment we'll deal with some of those common concerns. But let's just start with what the Scripture actually says:

- God the Father is the Lord of marriage, charging the husband and the wife with specific callings for their marriage (Gen. 1:28; 2:24).
- Husband and wife are to live together as coheirs of the gift of life, sharing equal honor and value as those made in God's image and as one in Christ (Gen. 1:27; Gal. 3:28; 1 Pet. 3:7).
- Husband and wife are to strive for unity and oneness submit to one another out of reverence for Christ (Eph. 5:21).
- In the same way that Christ is the head of his bride (the church), the husband is charged by God to be the head of his wife (Eph. 5:23; 1 Pet. 3:1).
- The wife is specifically made equal in personhood to her husband but is also charged by God to be the helper of her husband (1 Pet. 3:7; Gen. 2:18; the Hebrew for *helper, Ezer Kenegdo,* literally means "a helper who is corresponding to him" or "equal in power and ability to him").[1]
- The husband is to love his wife sacrificially, as Christ loved the church (Eph. 5:25) and as he loves himself (Eph. 5:28). He is to understand his wife and love her in ways that meet her deepest needs (1 Pet. 3:7)—for example, giving her security, valuing her

as an equal partner, giving her conversational companionship, and being emotionally responsive to her.

- The wife is to love her husband in ways that meet his deepest needs: giving him admiration and respect, providing him personal support, joining him as his recreational companion, and being physically responsive to him (Prov. 31:27–29; 1 Cor. 7:3; Eph. 5:33).
- Children are to be valued as gifts from God requiring time, sacrifice, personal attention, and training (Deut. 6:6–7; Ps. 127:3; Prov. 22:6).
- Children are to be raised to embrace a vision of changing the world and advancing God's kingdom with their unique gifts (Gen. 1:28; Ps. 127:4–5; 1 Pet. 4:10).
- The Holy Spirit is the conscience and the power that makes this kind of marriage possible (John 14:25–26; 16:8–15).

This is the biblical outline for marriage. Today, however, parts of it have become controversial among some Christians, especially the titles of *head* and *helper*. Many modern marriages no longer embrace these biblical terms or use them in their wedding ceremonies. Now, I (Shaunti) completely understand the impetus behind that trend and know that it is often well-intentioned (trying to omit anything that might be perceived as degrading toward women). But it results in eliminating a vital piece of guidance that is, when rightly understood, absolutely life giving and transformational to launching a couple into the loving, balanced, and *equal* partnership they are presumably longing for.

Today, as a result of avoiding or downplaying these awkward terms, many couples are launched into their marriages on vague generalities of love rather than with specific biblical responsibilities. The only clear mandate is that the husband and the wife must be viewed as the same.

The biblical marriage, however, is a radically different construct. Scripture recognizes first and foremost that men and women are created as spiritual equals before God. But as noted before, "equal" does not mean "the same." We each have our differences, including several gender-specific marital responsibilities. And the *reason* God gives each gender such a specific responsibility is not because one partner is inherently better or more able to lead than the other but because God is trying to bring balance, peace, unity, and abundance to a marriage relationship that sin will otherwise mess up.

But It Seems So Old-Fashioned, Even Dangerous!

If you are struggling with this outline of a biblical marriage (or, more accurately, struggling with the notion that a man should *ever* be considered "the head of" his wife), believe me, I (Shaunti) completely understand. When I first came to a true relationship with God and started reading the Bible at the age of twenty-one, I had the same disbelief and discomfort with this notion that many other modern women do. My worldview was already set, and it did *not* include a favorable attitude toward male "headship." Frankly, that idea made me furious! No matter how much my pastor or Christian friends tried to explain that God views women as equal, I couldn't get past how *unjust* it seemed, or the question of "Well, if we are equal, then why make *anyone* the head?"

Three years later something clicked as I was leaving for graduate school. My boss at work said he too was leaving; he and several colleagues were going to be equal partners at a firm he would head. A bit confused (I was still young!), I asked, "Well, if you're partners, how will you be the head of it?" And he said, "I'll essentially be first among equals. Ultimate responsibility has to be given to someone or there is chaos." And in that moment I finally understood one of the reasons for the biblical notion of headship. There is no such thing as a truly leaderless organization. Even in purely egalitarian partnerships, ultimate responsibility has to rest with *someone* for specific tasks. We've all seen how it works in equals-type situations like school project groups or volunteering efforts. To get anything done, someone either has to be given leadership responsibility by an outside authority or has to step up and assume that role. And like any other organization, someone in the family unit has to have ultimate responsibility. Chaos results when the family leader abdicates that responsibility.

Now that said, God has created the family to be different from your average business! In fact, unlike a traditional, hierarchical organization,

God wants the husband and wife, as equals, to always strive for unity, oneness, and agreement. This is not the same thing as "compromising to meet in the middle," and it is not, "I'll take your opinion under advisement and then make the decision, thank you very much." Instead, it is a purposeful effort to walk in true oneness of mind, heart, and purpose, including a willingness to defer to one another (Eph. 5:21). And as the one given the ultimate leadership responsibility, it is, in the end, the *husband's* job to create that environment.

Bringing Balance

You might be asking the same thing I did. "Okay, but why does God ask the man to lead and not the woman?" To us that simply doesn't seem fair.

The biblical answer is perhaps the most important and most misunderstood key to building the great relationship God intended us to have, which is why the selective use or ignoring of this Scripture is so tragic. The answer is that the head and helper responsibilities put us back into balance. A man's willingness to take a position of servant leadership, and a woman's willingness to allow him to do so, serves to reverse a man's sinful tendency to either passively shut down or to dominate, and serves to reverse a woman's sinful tendency to control. It brings us to true biblical equality—not the sort of modern "equality" in which one partner is, in reality, the one imposing their will on the other.

> It brings us to true biblical equality—not the sort of modern "equality" in which one partner is, in reality, the one imposing their will on the other. ℘

OUR TENDENCIES

To understand this more specifically, let's look at what each gender's sinful tendencies are. First, see what God told Eve would be the pattern for men and women after the fall: "Your *desire* will be for your husband, and he will *rule* over you" (Gen. 3:16, emphasis mine).

Our English word for *desire* doesn't come close to the full meaning of the word used here: *těshuwqah* is only used three times in the Bible. And we can see its meaning most clearly in the next use, Genesis 4:7, where God sees that Cain (Adam and Eve's firstborn son) has developed a murderous attitude toward his younger brother, Abel. God tells Cain, "Sin is crouching at the door; and its desire (*těshuwqah*) is for you, but you must master it." This word means a desire to envelop, master, and control. We see the desire to control when Eve decides to ignore her husband's God-given instruction not to eat the fruit and to convince him to do what she wanted him to do, as well. In other words, Eve in practice doesn't really prefer things to be fair, unified, and equal, like the rest of us, she really does want things done her way.

And in response to this controlling desire, Adam backs off, does not step in to strongly protect his wife, and becomes passive, just as is the case with many men today. ("Fine. Whatever you want.") The other pattern we see with men today (sometimes even the same men) is outlined in Genesis 3:16 as another possible and ungodly reaction to a woman's controlling desire: that a man may seek to rule. This is not the noble leadership God set forth for Adam in Genesis 2 but a cursed leadership that dominates, forces compliance, and demands submission: a rule of power, not love. It is an injurious rule men have used over women for centuries.*

The "desire to control" that God said Eve will now feel for her husband and the passivity and/or domination Adam will now exercise are both desperate and tragic. They are corruptions of God's original design of Adam as a caring head and Eve as a supportive helper.

---

*At this point, we must make a key distinction. While some men do become harsh and dominating in response to a woman's desire to control, that is not the only reason for that pattern, not even an excuse for it. A man's emotional or physical abuse of a woman is never "caused" by her approach. In fact, abusive patterns also often start with the reverse: a violent man partnering with a more timid or noncontrolling woman that he sees he can more easily bully.

SETTING IT RIGHT

So this returns us to *why* it is so important to embrace our biblical design of head and helper, not excuse, ignore, or change it. God knows each gender's sinful tendencies as well as what each gender is most longing for. As the chart on page 64 shows, He knows that our specific sinful tendencies will result in the *opposite* of what the other person most needs—passivity or domination instead of love and control instead of supportive respect. So the command God has given to each gender is *the one action* that will reverse that pattern and bring us back into balance and into the true oneness-oriented partnership God intends (and that we want). In summary:

What Women Need. We as women have a longing to be loved, protected, and pursued by a man who treasures us—and that includes seeing us as an equal partner.

A Woman's Sinful Tendency. Yet our sinful inheritance from Eve is to try to get our way, obsess over limits, and control.

What Men Need. As you will see in chapter 9, men most need to feel respected, affirmed, appreciated for what they do; and this includes the desire to "do it themselves." Above all they want to be the noble protector and provider for a wife and family.

A Man's Sinful Tendency. But a man's sinful inheritance from Adam is self-doubt, which manifests itself in passivity and spinelessness or in the tendency to "rule over" his wife in an authoritarian, unloving way (Gen. 3:16)—or both.

Do you see how this works? God designed Adam to be a strong man who loved his wife, protected her, and viewed her as an equal; but Eve's desire to control and take over leadership triggered his sinful tendency to back off, become passive, and check out. And God designed Eve to be an equal helper who respected her husband, but Adam's passivity triggered her sinful tendency not to help but to manipulate and get her own way.

God knows both of these traps are what woman and man will naturally tend to fall into and how much that will destroy the relationship we are longing for! So He gives us each the one responsibility that will, if followed properly, restore balance and result in each spouse receiving what they most need! Helper and head. In other words: Wives, let your husbands lead; husbands, take servant-leadership responsibility.

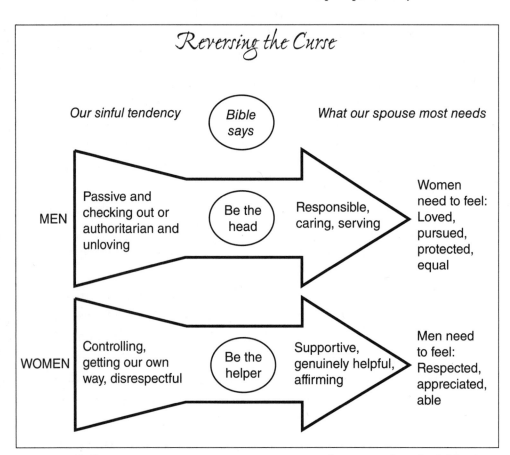

Before we move on, it is important to note that we realize the biblical pattern is not always followed properly and that some men will seek to dominate a wife rather than love and serve her. Although those situations go beyond the scope of this book, if you are in that situation, we strongly urge you to recognize that the biblical pattern of headship has nothing to do with dominance. Please talk to a trusted pastor or Christian counselor who can help you work through the next steps to address your husband's error. You also might want to read my (Robert's) book *Rocking the Roles*, which has more detail on the biblical pattern, as well as help for wives in dealing with husbands that don't follow it.

What Does Being a "Helper" Look Like?

So if we have this particular "helper" responsibility, what does that look like? Let's take a moment to examine it. In Genesis 2:18 we read, "The LORD God said, 'It is not good for the man to be alone; I will make him a helper suitable for him.'" The Hebrew word for *helper (Ezer)* is often used for God Himself, as a "helper" to mankind.

In calling the wife to be the helper, God is giving her the same type of role as He often fills in this world: being the one who could easily be the functional leader—and often is!—but who also recognizes that the most important need is not to "take over" but instead to support, build up, and help the person who has been given the final responsibility so they become the best person they can be.

I (Robert) think this is good news for husbands, for if anything is clear in life, it's that a man needs help. And the kind he needs most to succeed in life is one that is distinctly feminine. It is a help that receives, admires, nurtures, responds, supports, and loves. A man grows by this kind of help. He matures. He is strengthened to reach higher and do more than he ever could without it. The truth is, every man *longs* for this kind of help. And God has put in men something that longs for this help *from* an *ezer kenegdo*—a helper who is equal in power and ability to him, sees his faults, could do everything he does, and yet cheers him on and lets him do it anyway.

As a strong and equal partner, we as women need to respect our husbands enough to *let* them lead! *Someone* is going to be the ultimate leader of the family, and as we've seen, if the wife seizes that role, the man becomes either passive or domineering in response. But when the wife demonstrates that practical respect to her husband by backing off a bit, so he *can* lead, it propels him to become the loving, self-sacrificial servant leader to the family that God intends him to be.

We should point out that of the two different responsibilities given, the man's is far more difficult. Ephesians 5:23 says the husband must love his wife as selflessly as Christ loved the church and gave Himself up for her! That is almost impossible for any human being, but that is the standard

God asks all men to meet with their wives. When a man fulfills this role in the way the Bible describes, no one is happier than his wife. On the other hand, the husband who uses headship as a cover for control, condescension, dominance, or even abuse is not only *not* a head in the way the Bible sets forth but is instead a moral and spiritual failure.

Rightly understood and fulfilled, living out the biblical marriage does not result in male domination (the most usual concern) but is the pattern that will "reverse the curse" and enable our husband to be the loving, respectful, responsible, protective man that will delight us for the rest of our lives.

A Biblical Family

An extension of a biblical marriage is a biblical family. In a biblical family the husband and wife each take on the marital callings specifically described in the Bible (such as those listed above), and each will carry out all of the life callings that we'll discuss in the next chapter. But—and this is vitally important—the *way in which* the husband and wife live out their callings and roles will look different in each family. God has made each of us—and each of our families—wonderfully unique, with purposes that vary widely, just as our opportunities, gifts, and abilities vary widely.

The key is for a husband and wife together to determine *God's* wants for their lives, their marriage, their family, and to make decisions based on that rather than on worldly values—or even "church culture values."

This may also be controversial (in the opposite direction from before!), but sometimes some of the external messages we receive from the church and think are biblical are actually more representative of church culture or certain political views than what the Bible actually says. For example, how many of us have heard that the Bible says it is the man's job to work and the woman's job to stay home with the kids?

My (Shaunti's) former pastor at Redeemer Presbyterian Church in New York City, Tim Keller, is now a well-known author (*The Reason for God* and *The Prodigal God*) and Christian apologist. Described as a C. S. Lewis for the twenty-first century, he is widely respected among conservative evangelicals for being extremely careful to be biblically accurate. He really surprised us one Sunday when he preached a sermon saying that after years of examining the Scriptures, he didn't see "the man works, the woman stays home" as the biblical model of the family. He said that is the *Victorian* model, not a biblical one. He pointed out that (as noted previous) the *husband* is given the primary responsibility and accountability as head of the home. Tim concluded (and I'm paraphrasing here), "If any actual 'model' is presented in the Bible, it seems to be that *both* the husband and wife are working—often, together in the family business—and they *both* raise the kids. And the husband has the ultimate responsibility."

In other words, a family that fits into our "church culture values," where the mom is making the wonderful sacrifice of staying home with the kids, but where the dad works all the time and has little input into their lives, is just as out of balance—just as "nonbiblical," you might say—as a family where the mom works full time and has no time with the kids. It all goes back to both partners in a marriage ensuring that they *are* carrying out the callings God has for them—and doing so in the *way* God has planned for them.

It is so easy for us to seize on a cultural model that we see as beneficial for the family—which the stay-at-home mom model often is!—and call it *the* biblical model. But that is dangerous because (just as when we ignore "head" and "helper") we are trying to make the Bible fit us rather than fitting ourselves to the Bible.

After all, God's Word applies to all people at all times in history, not just those living a modern suburban lifestyle. Would we say that today's rural Chinese woman who brings in the family crops with her husband, while grandma watches the kids, is being "unbiblical"? Or the widowed aboriginal leatherworker whose children run and play with neighbors—or work with her!—while she fixes shoes to earn money to feed them that night? What about an ancient Middle Eastern woman who would make and sell clothes to earn income and help keep her household running—including to pay the live-in servant girls who cooked, cleaned, and watched the kids?

The Bible's truth applies to the time and culture of all these women—
are they being unbiblical? Well, actually . . . the latter example sounds like
a specifically *biblical* one: the woman lauded in Proverbs 31.

The point is: God has some specific callings and purposes for us
(which we will discuss in the next chapter), and we will each fulfill them
somewhat differently, depending on the unique time and culture God
has placed us into, the individual gender, gifts, and personality God has
created within us, and God's callings for our individual family situation.
*The biblical mandate is simply that we must fulfill them—and fulfill them in
a biblical way.* It is only if we *don't* fulfill
those callings, or arrange our lives and our
families in disobedience to God's design,
that we are being unbiblical.

> God has specific callings and purposes for us, and we will each fulfill them some-what differently.

And if we follow the Bible's pattern
and direction that *is* specifically set out in
the Bible (especially within marriage), then
we will be rightly positioned to receive His
guidance on *how* we as a specific indi-
vidual, married couple, or family are to fulfill those callings. We will also
be well placed to be at peace in a do-it-all world, as we work with our big
picture and individual design and callings rather than against them.

That discussion of God's core design and callings for us brings
together all the big-picture pieces that we have examined in the last few
chapters, and that will be the primary determinant in how we must shape
our individual lives. To that discussion we turn now.

5

Where It All Comes Together: Discovering Our Design and Callings

*I*n order for us to thrive in a do-it-all world, avoid regrets, and know that we are heading toward God's best for us, we ultimately need to understand what we were created to do and to be. There are three types of callings and design, which progressively take us from a broad picture to one that is individual:

- Our Core Callings: Our callings and design as human beings made in God's image,
- Our Feminine Callings: Our callings and design as women,
- Our Personal Callings: Our callings and design as unique individuals.

Where these three intersect we find God's best for our lives. *This* is the biblical road map that will, from this point forward, help you see God's direction in all the big and little choices you make in today's crazy world! (And then, of course, we have to have the courage to actually *follow* that direction, which is what part 2 of this book is all about.)

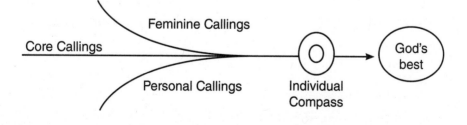

The Core Callings

Let's start by understanding the Core Callings shared by every human being because everything else pales in comparison to the importance of the overarching charge God gave all humanity. In Genesis we find three life purposes God has for every man and woman.

Before we dive into those, let's be clear that our ultimate, eternal purpose is our relationship with Him. God longs for a day-to-day intimate relationship with His children, not just as a Creator and a Master but as a friend (John 15:15). But that is not the same thing as the life purpose our Creator has given *to us*—in other words, what He has created us to *do*. And as both our "job description" and a major part of our personhood in this life, God has given all of His children three specific callings around which everything else we are and everything else we do as individuals must find its rightful place and order of priority.

These Core Callings embody God's timeless standards against which we can measure our life and to which we must adjust whenever we see that our life is not meeting those standards.

Each of us will apply the three Core Callings differently—and even differently at different times of our lives. But anyone who embraces these callings and pursues them as top priorities will order and manage his or her life in a way that is meaningful, satisfying, and, most importantly, in line with God's will.

We find these charges a few verses apart in Genesis. In Genesis 2:24, God said, "For this reason a man shall leave his father and his mother, and be joined to his wife; and they shall become one flesh." Genesis 1:28 recounts, "God blessed [Adam and Eve]; and God said to them, 'Be fruitful and multiply, and fill the earth, and subdue it; and rule over the fish of the sea and over the birds of the sky and over every living thing that moves on the earth.'"

In summary, God gives three major callings to the human race:

1. To leave and cleave
2. To be fruitful and multiply
3. To subdue and rule

Leave and Cleave

We are to become mature individuals who achieve deep,
lasting companionship in marriage.

Be Fruitful and Multiply

We are to raise up and launch a healthy,
godly next generation into the world.

Subdue and Rule

We are to advance God's kingdom purposes beyond the home
and into the earth, in ways specific to our gifting.

Leave and Cleave

The first Core Calling comes from the partnership of Adam and Eve as man and woman. This calling is about companionship—a deep, lasting intimacy with someone of the opposite sex in a superbond called marriage. No other human relationship can compare to it in either intimacy or durability. And, with rare exceptions, God has designed and planned for almost everyone to be married at some point in life. Statistically, more than 95 percent of women will marry at some point.[1]

Obviously this means that 5 percent of women will never marry. Others will marry but then find themselves alone again because of death or divorce, in some cases never to marry again. And still others will not marry until later in life.

Those who are single at the moment—or called to singleness long-term—have the same Core Callings as anyone else, with the exception of the second half of the "leave and cleave" calling. But the "leave" part still applies. All persons, single or married, must "leave" childhood behind and step out into maturity as the responsible adult individuals God desires them to be. For those who are single longer than expected, the "leave" process can be important as God uses the time to refine and polish a beautiful individual maturity in Christ that will eventually (in most cases) delight a spouse and be invaluable for mentoring others. And in the meantime, two and a half of the three Core Callings still apply.

In fact, as hard as undesired singleness can be for those who long to "cleave" with someone in marriage, God describes a time of singleness (however long it lasts) as a unique time of kingdom opportunity for the other two Core Callings. Paul wrote that unmarried people can leverage their singleness to give "undistracted devotion to the Lord" (1 Cor. 7:34–35).

Be Fruitful and Multiply

This next Core Calling—to be fruitful and multiply—refers most obviously to reproduction. Although there are painful cases in which people cannot bear children, most will become parents—either biologically or through adoption. But this calling means much more than to "have kids." Rather, God intended for Adam and Eve to reproduce "their kind" (Gen. 1:24–25). Each of us is called to be a part of raising up and launching a healthy next generation that will glorify God and bear His image throughout the world. That this is a part of what it means to "be fruitful" is clearly seen when the rest of Genesis and all of Scripture are taken into account (for example, Deut. 6:7; Ps. 78:5–7; Eph. 6:4). Children are an amazing gift that we are given to shepherd for such a limited time, and we must be so purposeful about using that time well. Calling a future Christ bearer into life is a breathtaking assignment, and it doesn't come easily. It demands spiritual authenticity, well-honed parenting skills, and a selfless attitude.

What it doesn't require is necessarily *being* a parent at the moment. If you are single, if you are married but don't have kids yet, or if your children are grown and off on their own, you can still carry out this Core Calling. You can find ways to speak life into the next generation by working with the children and youth at your church, tutoring kids in the inner city, babysitting for a single mom or dad who needs a break. . . . The options are almost limitless. It can also mean becoming a foster or even an adoptive parent. Many children in this world don't have loving, attentive, Christian parents, which gives you the opportunity to be a Christlike example in their lives.

There are so many amazing examples of this. One of my (Shaunti's) friends is Japanese-American, adopted at birth by a single woman named Betty, a missionary in Japan who wanted to give this baby the rare gift of a Christian home. She brought my friend back to America as an infant, then went back and adopted another . . . and another. Every few years she added another child to her beautiful, if nontraditional, family. When my friend was in her late teens, her mother sent her over to Japan to pick up her newest baby sibling. And then the others began taking turns, including helping other Christian families adopting from Japan. Today there are fifteen children in this beautiful family, all grown now; all raised to know and love the Lord and, like their mom, to be "fruitful and multiply" in reaching out to the next generation in need.

Subdue and Rule

Our third Core Calling is to subdue and rule. God wants all aspects of life on this planet—social, spiritual, and physical—to be improved by the hands of His people. Theologian John Stott said it this way: "God makes us, in the most literal sense, 'caretakers' of His property."[2] By using the word *subdue*, Genesis says the earth actually needs the rule of godly women and men if it is to be set right and made healthy, balanced, and orderly in the way God desires. And if this was true even in the perfection of the earth before the fall, how much more vital is this calling in a world that is deeply impacted by sin?

This calling does not just mean that we are to be good environmentalists, although we certainly should care for God's creation. Ultimately the subdue and rule calling is about advancing God's kingdom purposes *beyond the home and into the world.* It is about bringing God's light into dark places—whether that means via a formal ministry or simply by actively showing the light of Christ in our workplaces, neighborhoods, or communities. We are called according to our gifts and talents to the challenging tasks of helping people, improving society, enacting justice, sharing the gospel, and advancing God's kingdom. Jesus even taught us to pray this way: "Your kingdom come, Your will be done, *on earth . . .*" (Matt. 6:10, emphasis added). God has designed us for specific good works (Eph. 2:10). Just as the earth needs the cultivating hand of humanity to draw out its greater beauty, so too society needs the gifts of our hearts to make it better in a myriad of ways.

Rita O'Kelly has discovered one of those ways. Rita is not only an executive with a major investment company but also a kingdom builder. Despite a demanding schedule, she makes time to mentor a number of younger women in her firm before work and during the noon hour with her wisdom and godliness. She has helped a number of these women achieve more than bigger paychecks; she has helped them make wise decisions for their careers and families, overcome personal roadblocks, and find better balance and direction for their lives.

My friend Kim in my core group is fulfilling her subdue and rule calling in a completely different way. A single mom, she works a full-time schedule from home as a project manager; and on the weekends she enlists her little boy, her sister, and her friends on projects to help anyone disadvantaged by poverty or disaster. For example, this book is being written in the aftermath of the devastating 2010 earthquake that killed more than two hundred thousand people in Haiti. Kim recently spearheaded a donation effort that sent thirty thousand new and used shoes to a nation littered with dangerous glass and debris, practical help for needy adults and children flowing out of her love for Christ.

Or consider this example of Katie, a stay-at-home mom I met when she invited me to speak to a San Francisco-area neighborhood group recently. Katie had no formal, paid job, but she worked many hours for the kingdom. In an area of the country that is often suspicious of devoted Christian faith, Katie heads up her church's effort to "love our neighbors with no strings attached." For example, the members of the church will listen for and meet the needs they hear about at the local school—whether that means buying school supplies for a family who lost a job, or stopping by with hot meals when they hear through the school grapevine that an acquaintance has experienced a loss. The effect of this simple, loving care has been profoundly transformational in showing their community God's unconditional love: what a kingdom impact!

As with the Core Calling to be fruitful and multiply, the calling to subdue and rule and advance God's kingdom purposes can become a part of our life in an almost limitless number of ways.

Leave and cleave. Be fruitful and multiply. Subdue and rule. These three Core Callings together give us God's most foundational "purpose statement" for His children, and we'll talk about them a lot in the following chapters. For now let's move on to some more callings for us as women, as well as the personal callings we have as individuals.

Feminine Callings

In addition to our Core Callings, we also have callings specifically as women. As discussed in earlier chapters, we are designed as women for a reason. God has some unique purposes, intentions, and callings for us—specific reasons He made us women, not men. These are our feminine callings, which we have to understand and embrace if we are to find God's best for us. We are not talking about roles here but about what it means to *be* a woman and to live out that biblical definition of womanhood that we brought out in the last chapter.

I (Shaunti) have specifically looked for those Scripture passages that apply only to women and can be used to understand the unique female design *behind* the roles. I wasn't looking for a list of what women should do but why God was asking *women* to do certain things. In other words: what does a woman uniquely bring to the table that a man might not?

There are some fascinating answers in the Bible . . . and also in science. Today many fields of science, such as neurobiology and anthropology, reveal many feminine and masculine distinctives. Years ago a well-regarded, Yale-educated sociologist named Stephen Clark did a major study of how men and women act and think in all the cultures around the world today and through thousands of years of history. He would ask, "Regardless of setting, what if anything keeps defining gender?" I (Robert) was fascinated by Clark's book on his study, *Man and Woman in Christ*.[3]

Many cultures have tried to say that men and women are the same, and they tried to make them act the same. But Clark has found that it is futile to do so because throughout history, *over time*, men and women will always default back to their distinctiveness.

Clark mentions two long-term examples in modern times: the Israeli kibbutz and Soviet communism. Both structures believed that men and women are the same, set it up so they could *be* the same, and gave rewards if they *were* the same. Both did it for fifty years or more, and both were dismal failures. Both found, for example, that the women in the culture still instinctively gravitated toward nurturing choices, particularly around their own home. And the children and society suffered greatly from not letting them. Essentially Clark found that over time people default to their nature.

What Are We Designed For?

So what is uniquely female about our nature? Although many of these points are also backed up by science, what, in particular, does the Bible say about how we are designed? Let's take a look at five uniquely feminine callings. Some of these will sound familiar, as they are intricately related to our Core Callings and who God created us to be as women. This is not *all* we are designed for, obviously, but gives us a foundation as women that each of us will individually build on.

TO HELP (ESPECIALLY TO HELP) AND COMPLETE A MAN

First, as you saw in the last chapter, Scripture says we are uniquely gifted to help and complete a man, just as a man is uniquely gifted to complete and cleave with a woman. In Genesis, God looked at everything He had created and saw that "it was very good" (Gen. 1:31). But He looked at the man He had created and said, "It is not good for the man to be alone; I will make him a helper suitable for him" (Gen. 2:18).

We discussed this idea of women being "helpers" in chapter 4. Some women bristle at the idea of being a helper because they think it implies a lack of equality, but it doesn't. As mentioned in chapter 4, the Hebrew for *helper* is *Ezer Kenegdo,* which literally means "a helper corresponding to him" or "a helper who is equal in power and ability to him."

Most of us instinctively know that being a helper is the way we are designed. We see our kids or our husband struggling with something and we want to help, . . . and sometimes we get ourselves in trouble because of it! One woman at an event told me, "It's going to be engraved on my tombstone, 'She was just trying to help!'"

TO INFLUENCE HER SETTING

Second, in some mysterious way, God has designed a woman so that she is able to bring the influence of beauty, warmth, purity, and a sense of a "civilizing spirit" to whatever setting she is in.

Few situations can better illustrate the meaning of what God had in mind here than when a young bachelor marries. Go to his apartment or house before the wedding, and more than likely you will find a tasteless, colorless, Spartan environment. Just the basics . . . and a few electronic toys. There is nothing green or alive anywhere. The bedroom is dormlike; the bathroom, radioactive; the kitchen, unused except for a well-worn microwave oven. This is man *alone.* But then he marries. In the weeks and months that follow, his house becomes a home. Order, form, color, art, warmth, heart, love, and laughter fill what was once nothing more than a utilitarian staging area. More often than not, the man quickly falls in love with these startling makeovers. He had no idea until now that he needed this much help!

It's not just bringing beauty to his physical environment but to his life, his friends, and his jokes. Even grown-up, godly Christian husbands and fathers often seem to revert to teen-boy humor when they are alone . . . but add a woman into the mix, and suddenly they recognize the need for elevating their talk just a bit!

In every culture around the world, a woman simply brings a civilizing spirit. You've all seen it: there's simply more beauty and warmth and purity and kindness where a woman is than in environments that are all male.

These feminine-design callings are to be used wherever we are— at church, at work, at school—but interestingly God actually commands us to be *sure* to bring them to our home. Men are given many serious responsibilities for their home and children, but no Scripture commands them to bring beauty and purity to their home.

One of the clearest Scriptures that gives clues about our design specifications as women is Titus 2:3–5: "Older women likewise are to be reverent in their behavior, not malicious gossips, nor enslaved to much wine, teaching what is good, so that they may encourage the young women to love their husbands, to love their children, to be sensible, pure, workers at home, kind, being subject to their own husbands, that the word of God will not be dishonored." Let's focus for the moment on three of the descriptive words or phrases in Titus 2:5: pure, workers at home, and kind.

The Greek word for *pure* is *hagnos.* It means to be chaste, modest, free from defilement and impurities. As God is pure and beautiful, women are given a unique ability to reflect that through the purity and beauty of their lives. This is that civilizing spirit.

"Be workers at home" is the Greek word *oikourou.* This means "one who looks after domestic affairs with prudence and care." We are asked to bring order to the chaos that could be our home if we let it. This is a challenge for me (Shaunti), as my husband is naturally much more neat than I am, but thankfully, the Greek word doesn't mean "the one who cooks and cleans." It also doesn't say "because you are *limited* to the home" or "because women have to do the chores and men don't." No, the Greek simply means to "look after domestic affairs prudently and carefully," and there are many ways that plays out. But in the end it will *result* in bringing beauty and order and a civilizing spirit—something God says we as women are uniquely gifted to bring to the home and family unit. And that is incredibly important, as the Christian family is supposed to be *the* most important reflection of God's order to the world.

Third, the Greek word for *kind* is *agathos,* which in Greek actually means "good," or "full of virtue." Women have a special sense of warmth, kindness, and goodness that we are supposed to develop and offer toward others.

TO NURTURE LIFE

There is nothing more scripturally or biologically obvious than that women are designed with a unique ability to nurture life. This includes both physical life through childbirth and the more intangible emotional and spiritual life of those around them. I (Shaunti) fought against this idea for years. I knew our bodies were designed to produce children, but beyond that I didn't think we had any special purpose in that direction that is any different from men. I had never really absorbed how much both the Bible *and* science have to say about this.

But as I studied the Bible more and as I was exposed to scientific evidence that confirmed what I saw clearly in God's Word, it was clear: women *do* have some unique gifts and design in this area. We have a special ability to be empathetic and a lover of others, especially of a man and of children. Women have a relational strength of loving, nurturing, caring, and empathy at our core. Our brains have a structure and hormone mix that are even designed specifically for it! Men can *do* it and learn to do it well. But their brains are not specifically designed to be naturally great at it in quite the same way. In general, women are built to be good at nurturing.

Now, just to be clear: having a "natural" biological or spiritual gift doesn't always mean that the exercise of the gift *comes naturally*. For example, as a teenager I discovered, much to my surprise, that I had a good singing voice. That ability had been hidden until I took voice lessons and exercised it, and then suddenly I found myself in many elite choirs. Just as I would never have known I had that gift unless I did something with it, God has to *tell* women in Titus 2 to be "trained" to love and nurture and care for their husbands and children—implying that although He's designed us to be especially good at filling our family's need for love, we may not recognize or use that gift otherwise!

TO BRING SPECIAL WISDOM AND PERSPECTIVE

For this fourth feminine calling, we can go back to another of the descriptive words in Titus 2:5. Older women are to teach the younger to "be sensible." "Be sensible" is the word *sophron* in Greek. It means "to use common sense and discretion." Females have a unique sort of common sense and wisdom that Paul says must be fostered and brought to bear on life. The famous passage from Proverbs 31 says the ideal woman "opens her mouth in wisdom, and the teaching of kindness is on her tongue" (v. 26).

We women think differently from men, perceive things differently, and process things differently, which results in our bringing a different perspective. God designed us that way *on purpose* not to keep those thoughts to ourselves but to bring that different perspective and our unique brand of female common sense to the issues of life.

For years I have often found myself working in male-centered environments. I can give many examples of cases where if I as a woman hadn't been there, the outcomes or decisions would have been completely different than if the group had been made up solely of men. Women simply think differently from men, and our wisdom, perspective, and common sense are vitally needed—just as their perspective is needed in areas women might otherwise monopolize. Being one-sided in any direction will usually result in missing something!

Before we move on to the fifth feminine calling, let's highlight something about these first four. One word that sums up a woman's design in these areas is that she is an *influencer*. Take a look at 1 Peter 3:3–4, "Your adornment must not be merely external—braiding the hair, and wearing gold jewelry, or putting on dresses; but let it be the hidden person of the heart, with the imperishable quality of a gentle and quiet spirit (there's that civilizing spirit, again!), which is precious in the sight of God." Then Peter explains one example of *why* living out those positive and feminine qualities is so important: in order that unbelieving husbands *"may be won* without a word by the behavior of their wives" (1 Pet. 3:1). Our feminine design gives us as women a unique ability to influence what others do, think, and even how they feel about themselves. What an amazing responsibility!

> Our feminine design gives us as women a unique ability to influence what others do, think, and even how they feel about themselves. ❧

TO MULTITASK

The last feminine calling we should mention here is that we are uniquely gifted to multitask. You may chuckle at such a prosaic observation, but it is easy to overlook the incredible spiritual application for this gift: God created us this way because He needs us to use it to make life and ministry work. There isn't a specific *directive* Scripture on this, but we see many examples of this feminine design being used throughout God's Word, from Abigail rapidly arranging a massive apology gift of food to David's men, to Martha hosting get-togethers for Jesus and His disciples (although like the rest of us, Martha had to learn to avoid getting so lost in the tasks for Jesus that she missed their whole point).

Brain science makes it absolutely clear that this is how women are designed: our brains are literally wired completely differently from men in this way so that we can be thinking about and doing many "surface" things at once. By contrast, men's brains are wired to make them really good at doing or thinking deeply about one thing at a time.

One of the great examples of a female multitasker presented in the Bible is, again, the Proverbs 31 woman. "She rises also while it is still night and gives food to her household and portions to her maidens. She considers a field and buys it; from her earnings she plants a vineyard. . . . She extends her hand to the poor, and she stretches out her hands to the needy. . . . She makes linen garments and sells them, and supplies belts to the tradesmen. . . . She looks well to the ways of her household, and does not eat the bread of idleness. Her children rise up and bless her; her husband also, and he praises her" (vv. 15–16, 20, 24, 27–28).

No kidding, "she does not eat the bread of idleness"! She's too busy multitasking like crazy—running many business lines, doing volunteer work, and managing a household! Meanwhile her husband sits at the city gate, likely knowing he could *never* do all that she is doing, and he praises her for it.

Our multitasking brain is a gift, not a burden. It doesn't mean "we are the ones who get stuck doing everything" but rather that God has designed us to be *able* to keep many balls in the air! He intends us to use this unique wiring for the good of His creation and His purposes, including in each

> Our multitasking brain is a gift, not a burden. It doesn't mean "we are the ones who get stuck doing everything" but rather that God has designed us to be *able* to keep many balls in the air! ❧

of our Core Callings—and never at their expense. Like Martha, we do have to ensure we don't overlook the point behind the gift.

Feminine Callings in Perspective

The Proverbs 31 woman is also an example of how God's special reminder to bring this design to our homes and families doesn't mean we are *only* supposed to bring them there. We have a calling to subdue and rule the disorderly world outside our doors for God's kingdom purposes just as men do. But God says our feminine callings are very much needed in the home as the strength and foundation for what we and our family will do beyond our doors.

We believe there are many ways that our homes and our culture today are becoming rougher, less beautiful, more uncivilized, less kind, less nurturing, and less sensible because many women are no longer purposefully being that feminine influence God has designed. When women think we have to try to be more like a man to survive at home or to get ahead at work, our families and the world are missing something.

Our Sinful Tendencies

We also have to look not just at the positive side but also at the negative side of our gender. Men and women share the sinful tendency to separate ourselves from God and want what we want, but we also each have certain sinful tendencies that are common to our specific gender as well.

For example, we women have all these feminine gifts that make us great influencers, but if we're not careful, we can go beyond godly influence and into manipulation of those around us to get our way.

Similarly, we are designed to be helpers. But if we're not careful, we go beyond wanting to help and into wanting to control so we get things *done* our way. All too often our claims that "honey, I was only trying to help!"

aren't accurate. If we're honest, we were trying to make him do something our way. And this sinful tendency tends to trigger *his* sinful tendency to be passive and back off (or, sometimes, to react and become very angry).

And finally, we often tend to resist God's limits. For instance, have any of you felt that female bristling when you have heard Christian leaders talk about men's and women's "roles"? And how many of you are relieved when I say that our feminine callings are things we're designed to be good at but they're not what we are *limited* to? That is true, but it points out that when God *does* give us directives and actual limits as women, we have a tendency to focus on and obsess over the few things God asks us *not* to do, rather than the many things God asks us *to* do! Think for a minute about Eve. She was given every other fruit in the garden, but she focused on and obsessed over that one fruit God said *not* to eat rather than focusing on all the fruit she should and could eat! It is so easy for us to do the same.

Now that we have examined the design and callings God has given women as a whole, let's take a look at the unique design and callings God has for us as individuals.

Personal Callings

We will be covering the topic of what you do with your personal callings in depth in chapter 10. For now, here's our context: each of us is a one-of-a-kind blend of the specific gifts and abilities God has given to us, as well as the personality and temperament He has shaped within us.

Those two things make you unique on the planet, and God shaped you that way with a specific intent so you can uniquely bless the world. Interestingly, all human beings are 99.6 percent alike in our DNA. All the differences between us are in just .4 percent of us, and within that small percent there is almost unlimited variety as our personal callings and design flourish.

What gifts do you have? What is your temperament? What is your personality? As I travel and speak to women all over the country, I see beautiful people of every conceivable design—all different, all special, all with personal calling from God. I think about my sweet friend Susan, my best friend growing up. We were in choir and theater together, housemates after college, in each other's weddings, supporting each other through every conceivable drama. And yet we couldn't be more different in some ways. She gravitates toward life around the home; I gravitate toward being out and about. She has an amazing set of gifts as a homeschooling mom to five children—two of whom were adopted from foster care. My gifts are more naturally used on the road—often encouraging homemakers like her! She's naturally a quieter, go-with-the-flow person; my tendencies are, um . . . not. She loves scrapbooking, . . . and when I look at a scrapbook, I think, *Please just club me over the head now and put me out of my misery.* She thinks the same thing about my life lugging bags, books—and often kids!—through airports. Different women, different blends of gifts and callings—all distinctive. And all from God.

As always, though, each of us has a seed of sinfulness within us that can make an impact on our personal callings if we are not careful. Just as with any good thing, all of us have to be watchful lest we use our good, God-given gifts in unhealthy ways. Some of these concerns will be individual to you; they are those things you personally seem to struggle with most (for example, how easily my "life on the go" tendencies could come at the expense of attention needed by my family). But all of us share some sinful tendencies with regard to our personal callings.

For example, every one of us can be tempted to think, *It's all about me,* and take our unique design and use it to serve ourselves instead of using it for God's purposes for us. But of course, if we do that, where we end up won't be God's best. We're going to think, *I don't like this.* We will always be more fulfilled if we are willing to submit to the purposes God says are best for our lives and use our personal gifts for His glory.

What's Next?

You have seen how we need a biblical guide that will help us be "Life Ready" and not only live but *thrive* in this crazy, modern world. When we prioritize and arrange our life around our biblical design and callings as people made in God's image (the Core Callings), as women (Feminine

Callings) and as individuals (Personal Callings), we essentially build that individual compass or road map that will lead us to God's best for our lives. And then, of course, comes the most important part: we actually have to *follow* it. Not just think about it, not just agree with it—but actually take the steps that will allow us to thrive.

As You Move Forward

As you work through the pages ahead, you may be surprised how much courage is required to take these steps. It actually takes a lot of trust to follow a compass. By definition you only need to use it when you are lost and can't see where you are going. It is easy to want to follow our feelings instead. ("I know the compass says to turn right, but I'm *sure* its to the left . . .") It is also easy to default to walking the path that we already know rather than the one God is leading us to. Yet if we will trust God's biblical guidance and strike out on the road He lays before us, we *will* end up right where He wants us.

> It takes trust to follow a compass. By definition you only need to use it when you can't see where you are going. ❧

Doing so requires a willingness to dive into some personal applications of following this compass, to really examine our lives, and to courageously take several important steps of faith. Let's move to part 2 of this book where you will see how following God's compass will lead to that abundant life for *you*.

PART 2

❧

*Getting to God's
Best for You*

6

Living from the Inside Out

For many of us, our first step of faith will be the one that we have to be most consciously mindful of—at least at the beginning of our journey to find God's best. This first step flows directly out of our Core Callings as described in the previous chapter. The Core Callings are more than just a "job." We are *designed by God to fulfill them*: so in essence, they are also a big part of who we *are*. That said, these Core Callings represent only a *part* of ourselves and our lives—a crucial part, to be sure, but only a part. Much more than these callings makes us who we are. The relationship between our Core Callings and the other elements forming our unique identities can be seen in the Identity Circle below.

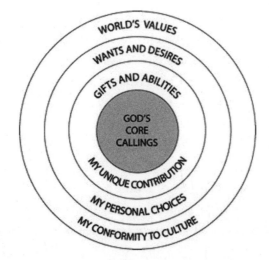

At the center of our identity are the three Core Callings. Then we begin to layer on our specific design as individuals—our personal callings. We come first to gifts and abilities—the unique ways each of us are designed—which include our design as women. This is where our lives expand beyond the sameness that covers all people, and we see those aspects of identity that make us unique—artist, athlete, musical, extroverted, high-capacity achiever, leader, administrative, numbers oriented, people oriented, encourager, helper, entrepreneur . . . the list goes on and on. This ring essentially represents the individual design specifications God has given each of us: built-in things we're just *good* at. If you do *The Life Ready Woman Study,* you will walk through a much more specific identification of those design specs, but for now, think about what that set of traits looks like for you. How are you built?

This is important because you are built that way for a reason. Your talents, abilities, personality, and so on are given to you for eternal purposes, and God intends you to step out and use those unique gifts as a light in a dark world. He doesn't want you to hide them under a bushel (Matt. 5:15). We will cover that in more depth in chapter 10.

Next in the Identity Circle comes the level where our wants and desires are found. God has given us all of these gifts, but He has also given us autonomy and free will. Here is where we define and shape our lives. What experiences do *we* want to have? What people do we want to be with? What dreams do we want to pursue?

At this level it's important to remember that the choices we make around our wants and desires have consequences—good and bad—when it comes to fulfilling God's Core Callings on our lives. Sometimes what we want to pursue and what we enjoy is something we're gifted at, but sometimes it isn't. To look at this from a business perspective, suppose a saleswoman might *enjoy* telling others about all the great features of the product she's selling, but if she can't close the sale, she is not fulfilling her job. So she might be more effective if she were to work in marketing instead of in sales. On the other hand, someone who did have the gift of "close the deal" persuasion—and enjoyed it!—would be great in a sales position.

Similarly, sometimes our wants and desires line up with the tasks, jobs, experiences, and commands God has for us . . . but sometimes they don't. This layer of the Identity Circle, then, becomes our primary decision zone as followers of Christ. If our wants clash with God's wants, we have to decide if we will live by what God wants for us . . . or by what *we* want for us. We often must submit our desires to God and allow Him to change them. Whatever directions our lives ultimately take, much of the unique script is written here by the decisions we make.

The third level of the Identity Circle, the world's values, is something we can't control. What we *can* control is how much we are to be influenced by it. This circle is where cultural forces seek to shape, manipulate, and form our lives into any pattern that runs counter to God's core design and callings for us—which many cultural patterns unfortunately do. This world around us is full of often unhealthy (and unbiblical) values wrapped in stylish images, and we are relentlessly bombarded with them through music, media, academia, and popular opinion. If these forces aren't countered by biblical values, after awhile they *are* part of what we want and *are* part of what we believe. It's amazingly easy to give in to them. We are told what we should look like; what standards we should embrace; how we need to arrange our personal, career, and domestic priorities; and what we should believe about manhood and womanhood.

Outside-In Living

It is all too easy to live from the outside of the circle to the inside. It comes almost naturally to let the world's values, our own desires, or even our God-given gifts and personality dictate what we do and how well we live out (or don't live out) God's Core Callings instead of the other way around.

To the degree we live from the outside in and let external values impact us, we will be hindering the specific, unique purpose God has for us. Recently, I (Shaunti) heard Dr. Ken Boa speak on the subject of his book *Conformed to His Image*. He said, "The more we are conformed to this world the less unique we become. We become a product of this world rather than a transformer of it."[1]

Instead, we must intentionally choose to live from the inside of the circle out, letting God's Core Callings order how we should use our gifts, what we do with our wants and desires, and how we confront the world's values. So the first Faith Step needed to follow our biblical compass is this:

Faith Step #1: Live from the Inside Out

This sounds so right and simple, but in today's culture living from the inside out often requires a proactive decision to walk the narrow road

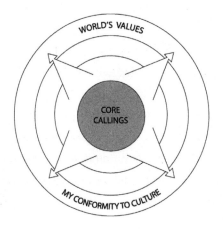

INSIDE-OUT LIVING

to which the biblical compass is pointing and *not* get sucked onto the cultural superhighways that lead to destruction. As you can imagine, *staying* on that narrow road also requires an unusual amount of alertness to maintain.

The hard truth is that in many ways many of us often live by the dictates of the world's power and influence. Even those who are spiritually devoted to Christ and who try to follow His ways often live this way without even realizing it! As we said, when worldly values almost seem to saturate the air we breathe, it's a current that's hard to resist without conscious effort. When we live from the outside in, the world's values and the cultural conformities that go with them will begin to dominate many things about us. This outer ring will squeeze and reshape all the inner rings of our lives into its mold. Our wants and desires, personal choices, what we do with our gifts and abilities, and our beliefs about the Core Callings all shift onto the tracks set down by the world's priorities. We are driven by our senses instead of by well-defined spiritual convictions. When we live this way, our core soon bears the twisted influence of the outside world. And when the outside world changes its values or presents new options and opportunities, we shift again, always working to make our inside fit the outside.

Outside-in living is also seductive and easy to fall into because it goes right in line with our sinful nature. We all know what it's like to give in to our sinful

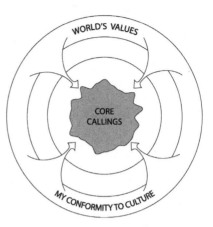

OUTSIDE-INSIDE LIVING

nature and do those things we know aren't right or within God's desires for us, yet they're what we want at the time. It works the same way, when we use our gifts and abilities in ways more consistent with the world's seductive pressures than with God's Core Callings.

Let me (Shaunti) share a personal example of how outside-in living happened in my own life, around the area of my children. I adore my two kids but did not start out with that innate, overwhelming pull or desire toward maternal nurturing of children that so many women have. Some of you will be confused by that concept, but others will know *exactly* what I mean. Deep down I felt more equipped and energized to be a leader to thousands than a mother to two. This wasn't a feeling that was formed just by the world's values but also by my personality, personal desire, and a skill set (or lack thereof) that all competed against my Core Calling to "be fruitful and multiply."

And to make it worse, the overwhelming blare of the world's values ("you can do it all!" "day care won't hurt your child," "it's quality time that counts") made it much easier to make little choices that progressively undermined my Core Calling. And eventually, not only was I not giving my kids enough quantity time; I wasn't even giving them that much-vaunted "quality time" I used as my consolation prize!

Through a painful time I eventually woke up to the crushing reality that I was hurting my children and the purposes God had for me as a mom. I began the process of learning how to reprioritize my life in order to live from the inside out—with my Core Callings as *the* starting point—rather than from the outside in.

Outside-In Regrets

The ironic thing about following the seductive pull of outside-in living toward a better life is that it doesn't lead to a better life! Outside-in living ultimately doesn't work. Instead, we experience problems and conflict. We may even experience lifelong regret. That's because by living from the outside in, God's Core Callings—which are what we are *designed* for!—have been compromised, dumbed down, or choked out altogether by a new set of worldly outside callings that are empty of real satisfaction (see Mark 4:18–19). Some Christians live this way more than they know and wonder why life is so troubled and conflicted.

God never planned for us to live from the outside in. Romans 12:2 says clearly: "Do not be conformed to this world." But since the day Adam and Eve rebelled against God, humans have gravitated to this kind of living. It has become our nature to believe the world's ways are better than God's ways. Outside-in living is often naturally our first choice.

But outside-in living exacts a heavy toll on us. It reshapes and molds life to fit values and attitudes that often run counter to our God-given design and calling—including the true femininity God has shaped within each of us. To try to go against this divine grain is an invitation to heartache. Our roots in Genesis shout this warning. Outside-in living looks delicious on the front end, but it has a deadly backlash. Just ask Eve.

There is a better way, and many women are living it. It's found in heeding a courageous call to live from the inside out. Nothing is more spiritually fundamental to our lives or as powerful.

This is not a call to withdraw from the world. It is an appeal to let God's Core Callings be your starting point in every area and in every decision of your life. Remember, these callings are divine commands, not merely suggestions. They are meant to shape your world, not be shaped by the world. They are, from a biblical perspective, the sacred nonnegotiables of your life. As such, they must be constantly in your mind to measure and direct (and possibly readjust) the choices and pursuits of your life. While you will certainly enjoy a wide variety of activities, interests, and opportunities that engage your gifts, abilities, wants, and desires, determine not to make choices at the expense of being true to your Core Callings.

Choosing to Live from the Inside Out—No Matter What

What if your life hasn't worked out the way you expected? Are you still supposed to live from the inside out? Of course. Sometimes where we are now may not fit the perfect white-picket-fence ideal that we associate with God's Core Callings or what we expected our life to be. We'll call this "God's ideal versus my real." But we still need to fight the messages the world sends us in order to live from the inside out.

What if that's you? For example, what if you are single and haven't been able to fulfill your longing to leave and cleave? Or perhaps you made choices earlier in life that have put you on a path that you realize wasn't God's ideal for you? What if circumstances have happened to you that aren't what you would have chosen? Maybe your husband abandoned you. Maybe you or a child got sick, and it changed everything. In all those cases, whatever your "real" is, if you are on a life path you would have preferred not to be on or one that you now regret, you can start from where you are now and still choose to live from the inside out. God will use and anoint that to steer you toward His best for your life.

Living inside out will look different for everyone, but just to give us one example, let's consider single women who haven't yet had the opportunity to leave and cleave. These women might want to look at two parts of living from the inside out. First, some women may need to evaluate whether they are doing all they can to ensure that they don't *prevent* leaving and cleaving from happening down the road. We've already talked about how some women are so excited about and focused on their career that they don't have the freedom to pursue a relationship . . . when suddenly they realize they have been *preventing* themselves from leaving and cleaving.

By contrast, one young woman in my core group, Julia, described a choice she made that went contrary to the siren call of the world, in order to prioritize a relationship that might be leading to marriage. Her boyfriend had not proposed, they had been dating for a year or two, and she wanted to go to graduate school, but all of those programs were out of state. So many people said, "You've got to do what you've got to do," and her professors were pushing her to go on to grad school. But she decided to wait. She realized that she would hurt the relationship with her boyfriend if she moved out of state and that seeing this relationship through needed to be her priority. Five months into our core group, she came in with a ring on her hand, so glad she hadn't listened to the world's advice. She could go to grad school in the future (and today, in fact, is doing so as a newlywed), but *this* was the key time for her relationship.

But what about the somewhat older single woman who was always open to being married, has made good choices, and would love to have a husband . . . but doesn't? Another woman in my core group, Angie, is in that category. The second part of living from the inside out, which is especially important for an older single who has tried to do it right, is to ensure that she isn't letting worldly pressure prevent her from fulfilling her *other* Core Callings and also to ensure that her disappointment doesn't stop her from continuing to be open.

Consider the story of a woman I met a few years ago from Canada, who has done something that many single women have not considered. Some might consider this controversial, but we think it is an important example to mention. This woman was my hostess at a Christian women's event who picked me up from the airport and drove me all the places I needed to go. She's in her late thirties, a successful businesswoman, and would love to be married, but she isn't. Like many older singles in the Christian community, the *reason* she's single is that she is refusing to live from the outside in; she is refusing to be unequally yoked or to live in a way that is contrary to God's standards. And as part of living from the inside out, she is adopting a baby girl from an orphanage in China. This is a girl who would probably either die or languish in an orphanage until the age of eighteen and then be set loose in poverty. Instead, this woman is giving this orphan a loving home.

Obviously, we strongly support the ideal of a child needing a mom and a dad. But millions of kids in the world have neither. A single loving mom can change a life, as long as the woman knows it is something God is calling her to do. But do not consider this option lightly. If it appeals to you, search your heart to be sure you are not trying to take matters into your own hands out of a lack of trust. Abraham's wife Sara didn't believe God when God said she would have a child, so she took matters into her own hands, and there were some pretty serious consequences to that action. So don't act out of a lack of trust. That's outside-in living, after all. But if you are in what you view as a "my real versus God's ideal" situation, pray about ways God would have you still fulfill the other Core Callings. And be open to some unexpected ways that He might guide you!

Women Who Are Living from the Inside Out

Take a moment to read the stories of a few women who have courageously made (or are currently making) their Core Callings their dominant reality and have successfully prioritized their lives around those callings instead of allowing worldly pressures, or their own desires or gifting, to change those callings. Your story will not read exactly like any of theirs, but hopefully they will give you encouragement to prioritize your callings to God's best for your life.

You probably remember the story I told of how the parents of Lucy, in my core group, implicitly taught her to value a career and independence more than having a family? This area of living from the inside out is one of Lucy's most challenging Faith Steps, but she is getting there. She is thirty-three years old, owns a business, and she and her husband have been "sort of trying" to get pregnant for the past few years. She knows she is impacted by the world's values, and she says her main obstacle is her worldly belief that "if I choose the biblical model or path—for example, to have children and pour myself into them—I'll miss out on something."

Lucy has begun the process of living from the inside out by talking about her fears with her husband and preparing her business so that it wouldn't fall apart if she decided to step away from it or go part time for awhile after having children. She realizes she needs to let go of the world's viewpoint and what other people will think about her choice to prioritize children instead of career. She also needs to prioritize her time with her husband instead of letting work consume her life.

So Lucy has made a plan of some specific steps to take in order to be true to her callings. She is going to make an appointment and go to the doctor to figure out why she hasn't had kids yet. She is also going to seek out an older Christian woman as a mentor and accountability partner. And she is going to set a time limit of ending work at 6:00 p.m. and spending the evening with her husband. These three simple action steps will help her avoid living from the outside in.

To give you another example of outside-in living, let me tell you about my (Shaunti's) former personal assistant, Leslie. She would get off work in time to be home when her kids got home from school. But before she started working for me, she also worked at a local retailer packing boxes and stocking shelves one day a week, and she kept that job even after she began working with me. She didn't do it for the money; she did it for the ministry opportunity. Most of the other staff members at the store were twenty-something singles with very worldly views. Due to Leslie's presence among them and relationship with them, she was able to provide the only Christian influence they ever encountered during the week. She was the only voice and example that was gently urging them to consider God's standards in their lives and to understand that God loves them.

When my ministry began to get particularly busy, I asked if she could work more hours for me and stop working that one-day-a-week job. I really needed the help! She prayed about it and told me she couldn't. Her other job was her personal "subdue and rule" ministry to a few dozen people who didn't know Jesus, and she was having an impact. I so respected her decision because it was a great example of how God was using her and because she didn't give in to the outside-in pressures (from me!) to spend more hours at the office.

Or consider the example of Sally, also in my core group. A popular television personality in South Africa, she could have had a great career in broadcasting once she moved to America, with her beautiful charisma and delightful accent. Her unusual gifts and her desires in that area certainly would have pushed her in that direction, and yet, she felt strongly that once she had children, she needed to spend their young years investing in *them* rather than in her career. Now that she has three young boys, she is a model of motherhood that many of us look up to precisely because she is purposefully living from the inside out and allowing her Core Callings to impact what she does with her abilities or her desires . . . rather than the other way around.

Then there's the journey of my (Robert's) friend Rebecca Price. As an outgoing, lively new Christian in college, Rebecca expected she would someday have a husband and children. But instead of sitting on the sidelines until that happened, Rebecca rightly decided to follow her gifting and passions and do something to serve God's kingdom. So after college she began a career in Christian publishing. Gifted with a good sense of what it takes for a book to succeed, Rebecca quickly proved her value. Her career expanded and with it came greater opportunity. "But all during that time I always thought that one day I would get married and have kids," she said. "Career was never my driving force."

But as time passed, the opportunity for marriage never materialized. Eventually Rebecca was faced with this question: Do I live freely as a single, or do I live waiting for a man? The answer from the Bible seemed clear: trust God and live freely as you are. Courageously, Rebecca embraced that answer and soon found herself being used in new and exciting ways. Doors for furthering the reach of Christianity through publishing opened on the West Coast, in the United Kingdom, and in Africa. Companies such as NavPress, Word, and Multnomah Publishing called on her expertise. And when Random House, the world's largest English-language trade-book publisher, wanted to develop a Christian imprint called WaterBrook Press, it looked to Rebecca to serve as the vice president of marketing.

Now fifty-five, Rebecca has begun daring new kingdom adventures with her friend Lisa Bergren, such as their first book, *What Women Want: The Life You Crave and How God Satisfies*.[2] As for marriage and children, those are things God has not brought into her life.

"I think one of the first questions I'll have for God in eternity is, 'Why did You not choose for me to have kids?' I have to admit that I really don't understand why it has turned out that way for me."

But this doesn't mean Rebecca is living with bitterness or regret. Instead, she has focused her life and her gifts even more intensely on God's Core Calling of kingdom building. "It was important to me to be content with what my sovereign God has called me to, and that is what I've done. And I feel blessed to see how God has used me and my singleness to further His purposes." One thing Rebecca wants single Christian women of every age to hear is this: "Don't take the short view. Women tend to do that and feel despair over not being where they want to be. Be active instead of passively waiting for life to change. By 'active' I mean pursue God, pursue love, and pursue excellence. Figure out how God can use you *now*."

This is inside-out living at its best. When we keep God's Core Callings in focus, ordering our outside according to our inside, life will increasingly gain momentum and freedom. It invites God's blessing. On the other hand, when we embrace the outside-in way of life, we are most often ordering up a serving of dead ends and regrets. We have all heard—or asked—the following questions. Why did I think life was all about me? Why didn't I take God's Word more seriously? Why did I wait so long to try and have children? Why did I relate to men the way I did? Why did I think my husband could make it without my help and involvement? Why didn't I invest my single years in something more productive? Why did I believe my kids wouldn't notice I wasn't there?

It doesn't have to be this way. But it will take Courage Steps of Faith to secure a better outcome. These Faith Steps are in essence the way you follow your biblical compass, steps to help you successfully navigate the challenging terrain of the modern world. These Faith Steps will lead you to a wiser and more satisfying life. The first of these steps—live from the inside out—is a great foundation for the other four.

So answer this question: how *are* you doing at living from the inside out? If there is anything you think you need to change, jot it down in the box now before you forget it in the midst of your busy do-it-all life!

"Is There Anything I Need to Change,
to Better Live from the Inside Out?"

_____

_____

_____

_____

Speaking of your busy life, our next Faith Step is about understanding your season of life and living out your Core Callings in a way that "fits" with that season. That is what we'll be discussing in the next two chapters.

Embrace a Big-Picture Understanding of Life (Part 1)

$\mathcal{J}$n Ecclesiastes 3:1 Solomon offers this succinct bit of wisdom: "There is an appointed time for everything. And there is a time for every event under heaven." We all know that there are seasons in life. And each season naturally carries with it certain unique characteristics, themes, and priorities, as well as specific opportunities and limitations.

We need not only to understand our current season of life but also understand *how* we can best fulfill our Core Callings in a way that "fits" with that season—and make the appropriate lifestyle choices to do so. This is, essentially, working *with* our design instead of at cross-purposes to it. Instead of feeling stressed and torn, we will feel like life *works*. We will feel settled where we are, as well as much better able to build and successfully unleash the next season. This second Faith Step is what we will be unpacking over the next two chapters:

Faith Step #2: Embrace a Big-Picture Understanding of Life

It sounds so mundane. But many of you—especially those who, like me, have kids at home—will find a seasonal focus to be revolutionary.

The key to embracing a big-picture understanding of life is to not get so caught up in what we want to do or *can* do today that we fail to look at our lives as a whole. Unfortunately (especially among younger women), it is all too easy to be focused on *right now*. We don't even think about the fact that some aspirations and desires are more suited to one season than another, or we mistakenly believe we can have anything anytime.

Take Evelyn, for example. Sharp and highly educated, she knew exactly what she wanted in a career: status, exciting assignments, financial security, and the freedom to make her own choices. The international law firm that hired her offered exactly that kind of future but at a price: long, hard work hours; 24–7 availability, being "dumped on" regularly by senior partners of the firm, and constant deadlines. It was the price of moving up. And in time Evelyn did.

She made junior partner by age twenty-seven and senior partner at thirty-eight. It was a thrilling ride that took everything she had, but it also delivered the future she once dreamed about.

Well . . . almost.

In her late twenties Evelyn became more and more aware of the men in her life. Actually, the lack of them. She had enjoyed a serious relationship the first year out of law school, but that failed shortly after she joined the firm. After that there was a long drought. At thirty-six she fell in love with one of her partners. After a yearlong relationship they married. Two wonderful, fun-filled years followed. But then Evelyn turned forty, and it hit her: she wanted a child. So did her husband, Jim. The only problem was they soon found that Evelyn's aging ovaries and lack of eggs had put this now deep desire out of reach. Even after spending tens of thousands of dollars on every kind of medical procedure possible, the answer always came back the same: no. It is so true that "to everything there is a season." Today Evelyn has the regret that she missed her childbearing season because she wasn't focused on the big picture.

Somehow many of us often have an unconscious defiance to the reality that God has appointed specific seasons for best addressing certain life concerns. We also possess a misplaced optimism that we can catch up later on anything we leave out now. It can be crushing when we realize we can't.

Research tells us that 85 percent of college women agree with the statement that "being married is important to me."[1] Yet many women make decisions that reduce the likelihood of courtship and marriage during the very season when there is the best opportunity for finding it. Instead, they pursue things like exciting and time-intensive careers, personal freedom, travel, or overseas ministry opportunities. Many of these pursuits are good things with godly intentions. I have talked to many women going or coming from the mission field, for example, who feel strongly that they are responding to a call of God on their lives. Yet the "relationship-related" thinking running in the background, behind these decisions, is the confidence that they will have plenty of time to meet someone. They assume they will marry later on. And for some that is what happens. But for others, when "later on" arrives, they discover that it's much harder to find a man they want to marry.

Now, clearly, if God specifically directs you to take certain actions—like going on the mission field—that might seem to limit your relationship options in a certain season, you do need to do what He asks, regardless. He knows how your life will fit together, and obeying Him is the most important way to find His best for your life! The key is to be sure you are considering and praying through all these things rather than making assumptions that may be in conflict with how God has, in fact, designed you.

Speaking of assumptions, research also tells us, "89 percent of young, high-achieving women believe that they will be able to get pregnant in their forties."[2] But again, the truth is that by that time they have already missed out on their primary childbearing season—ages twenty to early thirties. After forty there is at best only a 5 percent chance of pregnancy. And that typically comes only with costly, difficult, drawn-out medical intervention.

It is important to note, of course, that many women *do* instinctively understand and work with their season of life. In contrast to Evelyn's story, remember the story I told in the last chapter of the choice made by Julia, in my core group? She was pressured to go on to graduate school in another state since her boyfriend had not yet proposed ("Girl, you've got to do what you've got to do.") But she *knew* this was a special relationship and this was the best season for pursuing courtship and marriage—which would matter far more in the end than a graduate degree. She decided to put off graduate school for a year or two, and when Ryan proposed, she was so glad she did.

So when faced with all the day-to-day or big-picture choices, what should each of *us* do? In exploring the lives of many of today's most successful women, Sylvia Ann Hewlett summed up all she learned about these women and their life choices. She offered young women the following practical advice to help them avoid deep regret in the second half of their lives.

- Figure out what you want your life to look like at age forty-five, both personally and professionally; then live your life to that end.
- Give urgent priority to finding a life partner. This project is extremely time sensitive and deserves your special attention in your twenties.
- Have your first child before you are thirty-five.
- Choose a career that will give you both the gift of time and the help you need to achieve a work/life balance.
- Avoid professions with rigid career trajectories.[3]

Some may be quick to react to and speak out against these suggestions as regressive for women. But those of us who keep in mind the big picture of life will take the time to explore the wisdom of Hewlett's advice. Freedoms, opportunities, and responsibilities all ebb and flow according to the rhythms of specific seasons God has designed for life. Taking that into account is not regressive; it is *wise*. It is not like anyone is forcing it on you. Rather, a wise woman will make the personal, proactive choice to flow *with* these seasons, not against them. She will seek to discern what each season offers and requires of her; then she will adjust and focus her life to make the most of it. She knows if she does this, it will also help launch a successful next season rather than undercut it with poor choices.

Now, all this said, many women would love to flow with the seasons and have tried to make good choices, but don't find things working out the way they expected. If your life seems to be mixed up or stalled, it is *not* necessarily because of something you have done wrong or bad choices you have made. Even those who make good choices are impacted by living in a fallen world, including the poor choices of others. And sometimes God just has a different plan for our lives than what we would have chosen.

In the end we will not see the full reason for His plan, or the true rewards for our good choices, until we are at home with the Lord. Until that time we have to cling to God's promise that He has a plan and a purpose for us. We have to learn, as the apostle Paul did, the secret of being content wherever we are. There are positives and negatives to each season of life. No matter where we are, we can embrace our current season and focus on the positive things about it. Let's turn now to understanding each season in more detail.

Understanding the Seasons

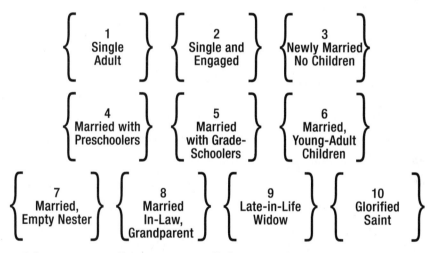

There are typically ten seasons of life. As you look them over, be aware that beginning with the third season—marriage—divorce or the untimely death of a spouse can greatly alter the dynamics of the seasons that follow. So can remaining single and never marrying, finding oneself unable to have children, or being a single parent. We will speak to some of these experiences in the next chapter.

For now we will look at what we might call the most typical or standard flow through the first five seasons of life. We—especially Robert, from his three decades in ministry as a senior pastor—will offer time-tested guidance for living wisely through each season. You may be tempted to skip to the season you're currently in, but we want to challenge you to read them all. Even though you are only in one of these ten seasons, you know someone in each of them. And as we'll discuss in the next chapter, part of our responsibility as kingdom builders is to help others during their various seasons of life as well.

Single Adult

In the movie *The Terminal* Tom Hanks portrays Viktor Navorski, an eastern European who is forced to live in the JFK Airport because while he was flying over the Atlantic, his home country ceased to exist through a military coup. He deplanes only to find that his visa is void and his money worthless. Worse still, Viktor is not permitted to exit the terminal and enter America, nor is he able to return home. He's stranded between destinations because he doesn't belong anywhere.

Single adulthood can sometimes feel a lot like that. You've left childhood behind, but without marriage and children your adulthood may feel incomplete. Your life is lived at an interchange. People come and go. Some befriend you. Others date you. But as time goes on, many also leave you as they move into different seasons of their lives. And there you sit like Viktor, feeling as if you don't belong anywhere or to anyone.

God invites you to see things differently. From His perspective the single years are alive with opportunity. The apostle Paul said in 1 Corinthians 7:32–35 that unmarried people are in some ways better able to focus on the things of God than married people are. Debbie, a woman in my (Shaunti's) core group, talked about Amy Carmichael, a nineteenth-century missionary to India. Amy wanted to be married and have children, but God didn't call her to that. Instead, she went to India, started an orphanage, and influenced countless children. Likewise, Debbie said, "My aunt wanted to be married, and now she's eighty and never married, but God used her in many ways. God calls us to different things, and the hardest thing is embracing that and saying, 'I don't like this, but this is where You have me now.'"

That is the key to *any* season of life. There will be times when you don't like where you are, where it is actively painful. But you can still determine to focus on the fact that God can *use* you in your season. And in many cases you are not there because you somehow "missed something" but because God in His inscrutable way has you there for a reason.

I (Shaunti) have a good friend whom I will call Lizzie. I have prayed for many years for God to bring a godly man into her life. But as the years passed and she entered her thirties . . . then mid-thirties . . . then forties . . . no potential husband crossed her path. She resolved to do everything she could do—she put herself in a position to meet Christian men, she developed good friendships—but nothing came of it. Instead of putting her life on hold, she said, "Lord, I'm going to trust You," and got on with going to seminary and her passion of ministering in Africa. While she continued to be open to male friendships, she resolved to work on herself. Then, in her mid-forties, out of the blue, she met a godly single man with a similar passion for Africa—and, eventually, for her. She had always privately worried that no man would want a globe-trotting wife and that she'd have to choose between her calling to Africa and a husband. But God knew better: although it meant years of waiting and struggling to trust, the husband He brought her in the end was far more amazing than anyone she could have imagined—and was a man who would fully share and support her in her Core Callings.

So let's look briefly at how your Core Callings play out in the single years. As my friend's story infers, the single years are a great time for character development, as you "leave" your parents and childhood and become a mature, independent adult. What sort of woman do you want to become? That is a good question for all seasons, of course, but it is *the* question in this season. What you decide here and act on will either serve or shackle you for seasons to come. Character is the ground floor of life. Who you are will always be more important than what you do.

In 1 Timothy 4:12 Paul said, "Let no one look down on your youthfulness, but rather in speech, conduct, love, faith and purity, show yourself an example of those who believe." Solomon's proverbs flesh out these general character traits with more specifics. Truth telling, generosity, sexual restraint, accountability, and a strong work ethic are only some of the items discussed in this wisdom literature. The point is that in your single years you have a unique opportunity to build your character rather than take on the harder work of *re*building it like many others have to do in later seasons. No one can choose your character for you. Character is intensely personal work. And it is work! As the historian James Froude once said, "You cannot dream yourself into a character; you must hammer and forge yourself one."⁴

So let's ask again: What kind of woman do you aspire and strive to be? Can you name the traits you want people to discuss when they speak about you behind your back? Realize that the better your character is, the better your life is.

As a single woman, it's important to spend time developing your abilities, including your career abilities. Somehow in some circles it has become taboo for Christian women to talk about career or world-impact aspirations, but the fact is, *every* Christian woman should maximize her gifts and potential to "subdue and rule" outside the home, whether she's single or married. After all, God Himself gave you that potential, and you never know how He might choose to use you. So let yourself go! Run free and hard into all the great things you can do and achieve. Discover the gifts, talents, and abilities God has given you, and use them to make a difference in your workplace, your church, and the world at large. Many of the skills and abilities you develop as a single will come back and bless you and others again and again in new ways in the following seasons. You may be surprised at the people and the opportunities that come calling.

You might want to use a number of the wonderful personality and vocational testing profiles available to help you identify both who you are and the gifts and talents you possess. Check out www.strengthfinder.com from the Gallup organization, www.aimstesting.org (Aptitude Inventory Measurement Services), and www.youruniquedesign.com. Each of these offers tremendous help in knowing yourself, your strengths, and what settings those strengths are best released in. The single years, from a personality and abilities perspective, are the best time to discover who you are, who you're *not* (sometimes this is even more important than knowing who you are), and what kinds of things make you come alive.

Take plenty of time to focus on your spiritual life. There are incredible spiritual opportunities for you to explore for growth and maturity as a believer in Christ. Don't cram your schedule full of empty busyness. Sure, you should enjoy life. See places, do things, go though doors that open only once. But put God at the center of it all. Link up with other passionate Christians and study God's Word together. Develop a consistent time with God alone. Use your gifts in serving others and advancing His kingdom. Make the most of your time and be watchful for the roles you can play in God's unfolding drama.

You also need to look for ways to live out your Core Calling to "be fruitful and multiply" by investing in the lives of young people. You may not have children yet, but you as a single woman can be an extraordinarily appealing and effective spiritual influence to young people of all ages. Consider how God might be calling you to reach out to children in your extended family, church, neighborhood, city, or on the other side of the world.

The single years are also the time to investigate and understand men in a very purposeful way—not just so you'll be "ready for marriage" but so you'll understand what men look for and need to begin with. I (Shaunti) have heard many comments about my book *For Women Only: What You Need to Know About the Inner Lives of Men,* but by far the most common is, "I wish I had known this before I got married!"

So read books and go to seminars that dissect the male personality, his needs, and his slant on life. Master the insights you find there. Become male smart and live from this informed perspective. Get past the stereotypes and the caricatures and find out what really makes a man tick, what most appeals to them—and what turns them off. Learn what authentic manhood is and discover how to judge a man by it. Know what to look for in a man before you find one of them kneeling before you with a ring in his hand and a glint in his eye. Remember this: the best way to find a good man and keep him is to become a good woman (1 Tim. 4:12).

Single Adult
WISE STEPS

- ☞ Develop your character.
- ☞ Evaluate and develop your skills and career path.
- ☞ Focus on your spiritual life.
- ☞ Find ways to serve and further God's kingdom.
- ☞ Understand the inner workings of men and your relationship with them.

Key Verse: 1 Timothy 4:12

Single but Engaged (or heading that direction)

Love. There's nothing like it, especially in this season of life when it glows red-hot. Life is now about "togetherness." It's a time consumed with drawing close. And that's where you need to be careful. Feelings often dominate this time. And though there is nothing wrong with that, it's important to realize that true closeness and close feelings are not necessarily the same thing.

Real closeness comes about only when two people value and embrace the same things. As the psalmist expressed thousands of years ago in Psalm 133:1, 3, "Behold, how good and how pleasant it is for brothers to dwell together in unity! . . . For there the LORD commanded the blessing—life forever." What applies to brothers also applies to marriage partners. Unity is life giving. No two people can live together in harmony very long if the deeper chords of values and beliefs are out of sync. And that is where the danger is. The intense feelings a couple have for one another during their engagement can often block them from exploring and dealing with these real issues.

For instance, are both of you in sync with God's purposes for your marriage? That's certainly one of those deeper chords. This question often draws a blank stare from engaged couples. God's purposes? In Genesis

God called the man and woman together to give them the three specific purposes we have already outlined: deep companionship, raising healthy children, and advancing His kingdom. To be married before God means forging a covenant together for aggressively pursuing these priorities and ordering life around them.

Of course, to do this requires a certain level of spiritual maturity and spiritual compatibility between you and your fiancé. That being the case, consider another deeper-chord question essential to your relationship. Are you both Christians? If you are and he's not, the Bible warns you not to move forward in this relationship. "Do not be bound together with unbelievers," 2 Corinthians 6:14 says. Why the hard line? Because the deepest language of marriage is spiritual language. Nothing draws a couple closer and keeps them closer than a shared spiritual life, and nothing is more likely to cause heartbreak later on than the lack of it. Therefore, be careful not to overlook or whitewash this vital area during your engagement. Be honest and ask tough questions. A broken heart or engagement now is far better than a broken life and marriage later. On the other hand, laying a common spiritual foundation will be the single most important thing you can do for your marriage. It will undergird every other season to come.

Take advantage of well-designed premarital preparation. See if a class or training program is offered at your church. If not, find one. And if all else fails, look for one you can work through on video or on the Internet. It would be wise to ask an older, successful married couple to join you in this experience. Interact with them about the information presented.

The point is: don't enter marriage unprepared! Most marriages that fail today fail within the first five years. On the other hand, research has shown that good premarital training virtually guarantees that this will not be the case for you. Make sure your premarital preparation includes large amounts of discussion, interaction, and practical helps over such vital topics as money, values, conflict resolution, marriage roles, marriage expectations, and sex. Another helpful tool during this time is personality testing. Personalities never change much. You can rub off some of the rough spots, but basically you are who you are. So the more you can know about each other's core personality—the strengths, the weaknesses, the pluses, the minuses, the needs of that personality, the language of that personality, and so on—the better.

Read a few good-quality books on men and marriage. Several we highly recommend, that are commonly used by pastors in premarital counseling, are Willard Harley's *His Needs, Her Needs,* Gary Chapman's *The Five Love Languages,* and my (Shaunti's) books, *For Women Only* and *For Men Only.*

Be intentional about making time for others during this busy period. It is tempting to spend much of the engagement period focused on the wedding, and having a God-glorifying, beautiful, special wedding is a wonderful thing. But beware of living from the outside in during this period of time—allowing the world's "it's all about me" attitude or vision of a perfect wedding to take center stage, dictate your time, and derail what should be the *real* focus: launching a marriage with your future husband. Julia knows about this firsthand. As you have heard, Ryan actually proposed in the middle of our core group year together, and as she said a few months later, "In trying to plan a wedding, all I hear every day is 'It's all about

---

Single and Engaged (OR HEADING IN THAT DIRECTION) WISE STEPS

- ॐ Embrace God's purposes for marriage.
- ॐ Participate in a quality premarital program that addresses marriage roles, expectations, differences, values, money, and conflict resolution.
- ॐ Know the strengths and weaknesses of each other's personalities.
- ॐ Learn as much as you can about marriage.
- ॐ Determine to live from the inside out.

Key Verse: 2 Corinthians 6:14

you. Do whatever you want. It doesn't matter; it's all about you.' And that's overwhelming because it *does* matter! And it matters what he wants, too. It's about *us*. At the end of day, we'll be married no matter what."

And as you prepare to "leave and cleave," you're not off the hook for living out your other Core Callings during this season. Seek God's will for how He wants you to invest in the lives of others and be His light in the world even in the midst of this busy time.

If all of this makes marriage sound like serious business, it is. It is joyful and wonderful—a dream come true!—but is not something to be taken lightly. Much of the happiness you will experience in life will come from it. That's the wonderful upside. So don't ignore learning about marriage even as you enjoy this high-intensity season of love.

Newly Married/No Children

You've trained, studied, sought advice, and looked deeply into the vital issues of marriage, and now the first thing you need to do as a newly married woman is *keep on* doing these things. Keep reading. Every year take a class on an aspect of marriage. Go as a couple to a marriage conference. Seek wise counsel when conflicts arise. This is also a great time for your husband to go through one of the Men's Fraternity curricula, such as *Winning at Work and Home* or *The Quest for Authentic Manhood* (www. mensfraternity.com). Like professional athletes, keep training at all times. Keep investing.

Today far too many first-time marriages end in divorce.* That means you will have to take your marriage much more seriously than much of the world does, and maybe even more seriously than your parents did. Seek third-party support for your young marriage. Find a couple who has been in the marriage game longer than you. Go to this husband and wife for

---

*Contrary to what you might see in the media, the divorce rate is not 50 percent. In fact, no one knows the exact divorce rate since the government stopped tracking the necessary data in 1996. Depending on the study, the divorce rate appears to be around 40 percent or slightly higher for first-time marriages in general and around 25 to 30 percent for regular churchgoers. See endnote 5 in this chapter for information on those studies.

advice. Open your life. Drain tension. Get wisdom. Make them your life coaches. Let them peer in through the windows to your soul. Let them ask hard questions. It will feel invasive at first, but remember that windowless lives almost always have trouble. Don't close yourself off from the help available.

It's also vital to create some firm financial disciplines early in your marriage to which both of you agree and adhere. You'll probably both be working, so develop your abilities and gain confidence and experience in a career path. Establish yourself. Remember, what you gain from work now can be leveraged in other seasons of life as something to fall back on or as something with which to open new doors. Make the most of it.

But be careful with the money you make as a couple. A double income is seductive. You can overbuy, overextend, and destabilize your marriage. You can quickly become enslaved to financial obligations and commitments (car payments, mortgages, and loans) that demand you work even during seasons when you long to be home.

In sober point of fact, couples often make long-term financial decisions while in this first stage of married life that have either positive or negative implications for all of the subsequent stages. So take those implications into consideration from the start. In addition, consider these very important questions and make a plan around the answers: Will you and your husband both continue to work long term? What about if/when you have children? Full-time? Part-time? What about one or both of you scaling back or working from home? Is that possible? If so, at what point will you potentially transition from two incomes to one?

No matter what you decide, it needs to be a *team* decision between you and your husband that's made after careful consideration of God's Word, your unique situation, and what's ultimately best for your family.

A radical and wise step would be to live on one income from the start. My (Robert's) wife and I did that. Every month we put her entire salary into savings. We knew when kids came along she would want to stay home with them while they were young. So we purposely lived a one-income lifestyle from the beginning. We bought used cars and limited our purchases.

Newly Married with No Children
WISE STEPS

- Continue expanding your marriage skills.
- Set clear financial boundaries.
- Plan for your family financial / career strategy once you have children.
- Identify and develop common fun activities.
- Make the most of your opportunities.
- Use your gifts and abilities to minister to and invest in others.

Key Verse: Ephesians 5:31

What we really desired in this opening season of our marriage was not stuff but rich—and *fun*—experiences together. Some of the money we saved during this time gave us this opportunity in a big way. After a year of disciplined living, we made a memory most couples only dream about for their retirement. We packed our bags and took off to Europe and the Middle East. We rode camels to the pyramids, sailed down the Nile under moonlight, scampered up the Eiffel Tower like teenagers, stood on the Mount of Olives overlooking Jerusalem, and walked the shores of Galilee. That was nearly forty years ago, and we haven't stopped talking about it yet. It created in both of us a love of travel that has now become our common fun. As for the new car we didn't buy in those early days, well, we haven't missed it once.

Finally, get involved together in a local church. Build a Christian community around you, and don't give in to the myth that "divorce is just as likely among churchgoers." Research shows that couples who attend church together on a regular basis are at least 35 percent less likely than all other Americans, including infrequent churchgoers, to get a divorce.[5]

During this season of life, you may be tempted to focus solely on yourself and your new husband. Don't get us wrong, it's great to spend a lot of quality time with your spouse. But even if you don't yet have children, you still have the Core Calling of being fruitful and multiplying. Invest in kids and teens who need wise mentors. Use your gifts and abilities to further God's kingdom in the ways He has called you personally.

Married with Preschoolers

Have you ever seen the bumper sticker that says, "My children saved me from toxic self-absorption"? There's a lot of truth in that. If ever there was a season of life that is not about you, this is it. Your little ones require major-league attention. They are desperate for face time with you.

I (Robert) once read a story about a young third-grader named Timmy who was having trouble at school. Timmy's mother was called in to discuss his poor performance. She heard about his reading problems and his struggles with math. Then the teacher asked, "Why does Timmy always say, 'Love is slow'?" Timmy's mother suddenly began to sob. She knew. She then explained about her demanding job and the long hours she had to give to it. To get to work on time in the morning, she constantly had to push Timmy along. Then at night after a long day, she had to rush back home to cook dinner, clean up, and get to bed. The whole time she was pressing Timmy to finish his homework, pick up his toys, take a bath, and so on. "I find myself constantly saying to him, 'Timmy, you are so slow!'"

For any child love is slow. Children need large amounts of time and focused attention. That's particularly true for children five years of age and younger. But for whatever reasons, today it's very hard for many young parents to hear that. And even when we are physically with our children, it is amazingly easy not to be *with them*.

When I (Shaunti) first began fighting my workaholic tendencies, I thought I was doing well by creating a part-time work schedule. Sure, my "Mommy time" would be interrupted by some cell-phone calls and e-mails but no biggie, right? Wrong. I finally woke up to the importance of *focused* attention when we would get in the minivan and start driving . . . and my three-year-old son would plaintively say, "Mommy, take your ears off." He saw my Bluetooth headset go on my ear, and in his little heart he knew

Mommy's attention was not on him. And he, like all small children, *needed* the attention of his mom and his dad.

In a recent landmark study conducted by Dartmouth Medical School, researchers discovered that the way a child's brain wires itself, neurologically speaking, is actually determined *after* birth by the care and attention he or she receives. *Love* shapes a child's brain! Love helps a child's brain connect itself together in a healthy way. The Dartmouth study also found that if a child is neglected and the love he or she needs falls short, these same neurological connectors actually *mis*connect, creating emotional and intellectual deficits in the brain that can last a lifetime.[6]

New sociological data backs up these findings. It shows that as the economy and standard of living in America has skyrocketed in the past thirty years, so has the rate of mental disorders and emotional problems among children.[7] It's an epidemic money doesn't fix. Nothing is more indispensable to a young child than large amounts of time and attention from a loving mother *and* father.

Your spouse needs you too in this season of life. A lot of the things that were fun when you first married—spontaneity, freedom, and extra money—are simply gone now, banished by a teetering pile of diapers,

---

Married with Preschoolers
WISE STEPS

☞ Be there for your children.
☞ Keep time for your marriage.
☞ Avoid major debt.
☞ Carefully evaluate your and your husband's careers.
☞ Look for child-friendly ways to "subdue and rule."
☞ Seek ways to use your gifts.

Key Verse: Titus 2:4–5

sleepless nights, calls to "Watch me," and growing pains. This is a major marriage adjustment time.

That being said, you must keep time for your spouse. This will not be easy. Early childhood parenting is exhausting, but don't allow it to eclipse your marriage. The best survival remedy I (Robert) know is the one my wife Sherard and I practiced for years in this season of our lives: we took quarterly getaways together. These can do what the frenzy of everyday life at this stage cannot do: provide you with some much-needed downtime when you can rest and focus on one another. You may not have a lot of money for this, but a special overnighter (or more) once every three months will serve as an oasis of refreshment for you and your husband to talk, reflect, plan, play, and romance. And don't call home either. Make it a clean break. The kids will be okay.

In this stage you'll also need not only to be a careful steward of your finances (a theme in every stage of life) but to implement the plans you came up with *before* you had children about what you would do once you actually had children!

You do not need to put your life on hold during this season (or any other season, for that matter). In fact, many of you can't do so. Take my (Shaunti's) core group member Lucy, for example. If she puts her graphic design business on hold while her kids are small, what happens to the business and the employees who count on her for a job? Another group member, Sally, *did* make the decision to leave an exciting career in broadcasting for a time to be a stay-at-home mom while her kids are young. But as she astutely put it, "It's not about putting our lives on hold. It's more like thinking about it in advance and establishing a conviction ahead of time that lines up with the Bible so that *when* you go into that season God will enable you to handle it in line with Scripture rather than just respond."

That's why we need a big-picture perspective on life. We need to make wise choices in the season we're currently in, but we also need to look ahead to the next season and see how we can prepare for it.

During this time of your life, you will likely be focused on your Core Calling to be fruitful and multiply, as well as (hopefully) to leave and cleave. But don't forget that third Core Calling—to subdue and rule. We know you're busy, but this calling doesn't need to be separate from the others. If you have a job, you can share Christ's love with your coworkers. If you "stay home," you're not really home all the time, right? You're often out and about with your kids and have a lot of interaction with other parents of preschoolers, the workers at the library, the YMCA, and so forth. You still have plenty of opportunities to be a Christian witness in your world *and* to steward your God-given gifts from an eternal perspective. Even though (for most women) how you do that will almost certainly look different from others during this season.

Married with Grade-Schoolers

This is an odd time for a woman. I (Shaunti) can say that since this is my current season of life! In some ways you feel you're able to ratchet down your commitment level. No more diapers. You're sleeping again. The kids can bathe and dress themselves just fine. You breathe a little easier.

Or do you?

The fact is, you might find yourself ramping up your efforts as never before. You run the kids from school to soccer to baseball to tutoring to the overnighter at the Joneses' place. You do parties, recitals, and school plays. And on top of all of that, you might (like me) also hold down a part-time or full-time job.

During this season many moms who are working begin to feel, as never before, that they're missing some of those special moments in their children's lives. There are simply not enough hours in the day, and trade-offs are naturally being made.

Other mothers begin to entertain the idea of going back to work as their children grow older. But how much work? There are no easy answers or formulas. It is important in this season constantly to assess the work-home dynamic.

This is true not only for you but also for your husband. Although God has wired men to say, "I love you," through being a provider, children ultimately need their father's presence just as much his income! Many couples today (like us) have together chosen a trajectory that allows the husband to also have a more flexible work schedule during these years so he can step into the all-important role of speaking life into his children with plenty of time together. In our cul-de-sac, for example, one dad leaves for his corporate job at 5:30 a.m. in order to be home by 5:30 p.m. to coach his kids' baseball teams; another runs a design company's finances with his focus on flexibility for half or full days off to drive his teenage daughter to softball tournaments around the state. In our house Jeff has kept his start-up company going instead of returning to a big law firm so he can be the one to pick the kids up at school when mom is on a speaking trip. (My kids call it "Camp Dad." I think he's more fun than I am!)

The key, as in other stages of life, is prayerfully to determine *together* what God would have you and your husband do during these years. If you're not sure about your balance, ask your kids! They will undoubtedly have an opinion about the amount of time you and your husband spend at home and at work.

Financially, both income and expenses will probably keep rising in this season. You'll find it's extremely easy to spend more money than you make and nearly impossible to save too much. How are you and your husband dealing with your finances in this season of life? If you're having trouble making ends meet or saving toward college or retirement, consider meeting with a financial counselor or going through a biblically based course on financial management.

Married with Grade-Schoolers
WISE STEPS

- Assess your and your husband's work-home balance.
- Get serious about financial stability.
- Adjust your parenting according to each child's particular personality and gifts.
- Explore kingdom work in which you can invest your abilities.

Key Verse: Proverbs 22:6

Next, as your children move through their school years, their unique personalities and talents should become more and more apparent. We cannot stress enough how important it is for both you and your husband to recognize and honor who your child is and what gifts and abilities he or she possesses. (And again, the only way to do that is to have a lot of time together and to take time to explore their interests.) Don't overlook or play down talents that seem odd or undesirable to you. Play up your child's gifts! And don't try to make children what they're not. Don't try to make a musician an athlete or push your easygoing kid to be an aggressive goal setter. Let them be themselves, whatever course that takes. Make them feel special because of their gifts.

Proverbs 22:6 says, "Train up a child in the way he should go." A more literal translation would be, "Train up a child according to his bent." Know and honor this bent, and encourage your child to grow and flourish. In that regard, consider doing some basic personality and gift testing in order for you to have an objective appraisal of your child's gifts and abilities. This becomes very helpful in knowing how to influence your child's life as he or she moves through school, especially through junior high and high school. (For example, see the "Strengths Explorer" guide for youth from Gallup.)

Again, find ways to use your gifts and abilities to invest in the lives of others, minister to those in your community, and "subdue and rule" in the ways God leads you. I know some of you are thinking, *Is it really possible to use my gifts and abilities for anything outside my family during these hectic years? I want to, but I feel like maybe I shouldn't, even if I had time. I should only be focused on my family, right?* Wrong! Again, let's look to my (Shaunti's) core group member Debbie for an example. "I love theater but thought when I had kids that I had to switch to making pillows. That was the mommy thing to do. . . . But my husband said, 'You're still a theater person. You can do that!' and God has given me so many opportunities to work with theater and directing." You, too, can use your gifts in many ways even during this busy season of life. Just seek the Lord to see how He wants you to steward your gifts and follow your personal callings during this season.

Keep Sight of the Big Picture

So are you starting to see how the "big picture" unfolds with the first five seasons of life and the fact that "there is a time for every event under heaven" (Eccl. 3:1).

The next chapter will address the next five seasons and will also dive into the discussion of those many cases where our lives don't always progress neatly down the "standard" path.

8

Embrace a Big-Picture Understanding of Life (Part 2)

$\mathcal{I}$n the previous chapter we began looking at the "early" seasons of life. Now let's outline the rest of them.

We will also discuss the many exceptions to this seasonal progression and summarize our main takeaway for what the seasons concept means for our Core Callings.

The Rest of the Seasons of Life

Married with Teenager/Young-Adult Children

You've taken your kids through "Ready" and "Set." Now it's time for "*Go!*" Like it or not, your teenage children increasingly need their own space. As emerging adults, they are in the serious business of defining their own lives, and they must do this more and more without you. This means you must gradually transition from your role as chief caregiver, guardian, and standard-bearer to a role that more resembles a counselor, consultant, and, once they hit true adulthood, a friend.

During the early teen years, you may find that you suddenly have to plan for even *more* focused attention in time, energy, and wisdom as they stretch their wings, taste freedom for the first time, and develop new friendships and ways of thinking. I (Shaunti) saw this necessity over and over in my research with teens for *For Parents Only*. But as they approach the age of eighteen and the possibility of leaving home, the process of walking along-side their decisions (rather than making them) becomes more urgent.

As a pastor, I (Robert) can confirm that this can be difficult for many moms. It's natural to want to maintain a close, protective orbit around your kids' lives, but doing so will do more harm than good. You'll exhaust everyone if you try to preserve unmodified that original type of bond you had with your kids. Yes, they need a mother for life, but what they don't need is *mothering* for life. That can actually harm your kids—especially sons.

When a mom refuses to let go of her son but instead overnurtures and overmothers him, one of two negative things may happen. First, she may inadvertently train her son to fear closeness with a woman. That's because closeness to mom brought with it her control and smothering love. Therefore, for his masculinity and sense of autonomy to survive, the son must constantly push his mother away and rebel against her excessive involvement. But in doing so, he also learns at this impressionable age to fear *all* feminine love as a threat to self. Later as adults, men like this can successfully relate only to women they can dominate. No giving in. No compromise. No getting too close. No talking back. Just do as I say. This is how such men feel safe with women. It's a survivalist tactic they learned at home in their relationship with mom.

Married with Young-Adult Children
WISE STEPS

- ☞ Change parenting style to release children into adulthood.
- ☞ Establish a long-range financial plan.
- ☞ If you stayed home before, possibly go back to work.
- ☞ Find kingdom work that excites you and uses your skill set.
- ☞ Make time for special marriage getaways.

Key Verse: Proverbs 31:10–27

Alternatively, a mother who won't let go of her son may breed an overly feminized man. Rather than fight against his mother's control, this son instead wholeheartedly embraces it and lets it rob him of his emerging manhood. For that, he will remain a boy emotionally even as he grows into a man physically. Instead of leading and caring for the women in his life, he will look to them to do these things for him—exactly as mom did. Today America is full of such men. They are soft, passive, noninitiating males who have lost the will to be men because they yielded to moms who loved and cared (or controlled) too much to let them grow up.

The wise mother understands that her God-given mandate is to prepare her children for autonomous living. Family relationships are never meant to be broken, but the emotional umbilical cord tying mother and child so tightly together has to be cut in this season of life.

Then there's work. If you have been a stay-at-home mom, now might be the time for you to consider reengaging your career or actively seeking out more time-intensive subdue-and-rule kingdom-building opportunities. With your teenagers preparing to leave home or entering college and with growing needs for extra income and retirement savings, stepping back into part-time or full-time income-earning work may be a wise move. If you've been away from the workplace or ministry arenas for a while, no doubt your first steps will feel tentative and untrained, but courage and diligence can move you forward again. You might think of the Proverbs 31 woman in this context. She certainly cared for her family's needs, but she was also industrious in other spheres.

You also have the chance at this time to spread your personal wings dramatically and explore your individual gifts in new ways. This might also start the process of crafting a new vision for the next seasons of your life.

Some women may even have the financial freedom to forego a career. For you there is the opportunity to consider instead a new and more expanded phase of kingdom work. Maybe you will volunteer your skills at church, at a school, at a local faith-based agency, or in a ministry on the other side of the world! Yes, you *can* do that. Mentor young women, tutor struggling students, serve on the board of a nonprofit, do charity fund-raising, help plant a new church, develop a Christian drama team, do financial counseling, work in a recovery program, develop and oversee your church's Web site, work with international students, or lead your own ministry organization. It's your life. Make it an adventure!

This is also the time to enjoy life with your husband in new and exciting ways. For example, in this season Sherard and I decided to sell our house and buy another one we could remodel together after the kids were gone. We made it *our* project *for us*. We also took several exotic vacations—just the two of us. With extra time and with your teenagers often consumed with their own agendas, the opportunity is there to step out in new and bold ways. So go for it!

Married Empty Nester

An amazing thing happens when the last kid packs up and leaves the house: you and your husband start dating again. You rediscover the movie theaters and restaurants that mysteriously fell off your map decades ago. You sleep in, eat out, stop over, and drive on and on to wherever the scenic road leads. This is a time for marital revitalization. Or at least it should be! With the kids gone, the opportunity is there to forge new goals and plan new adventures together. Don't miss this opportunity, or you will miss each other.

I (Robert) remember talking with one empty-nester friend of mine who surprised me with the announcement that he had recently purchased a motorcycle. "It's time to ride!" he bellowed. I laughed as I pictured my friend—a quiet, humble physician—morphing into a wild, carefree biker roaring down the highway. Then I asked, "What did your wife think about your buying a motorcycle?" He paused for a moment and then with a boyish grin said, "She bought one too." Now there's a wise couple. They could have each done their own thing, but instead they chose to spend time together doing something new and different.

This season is also a time to compose new and exciting individual goals. Really, your "subdue and rule" and career options are wide open now. You can restart your former career or ramp it up to a new level of commitment, and do so with the satisfaction that you've been the mom your children needed. Or you might dare to take up the challenge of an entirely new pursuit. You could try your hand at art, teaching, administration, caregiving, leadership, or even something as bold and meaningful as what Lisa Smith and her husband, Frank, did.

Lisa and Frank had truly arrived. After twenty years of hard work and faithfulness, they had established themselves as pillars in their church, their community, and their workplaces. Best of all, they had succeeded in raising their two sons to follow Christ. As for finances, they had practiced careful stewardship with everything God gave them. Now they were middle-aged and debt free. With a household income well into six figures, they had the freedom to buy the toys they'd always dreamed of—a boat, luxury cars, or a beachside condo—all of these things were real possibilities now that the children were all grown up.

So what did they do? They sold their big house and all their furniture. *All* of it. Time for bigger and better, right? Well, yes. Freshly relieved of all their property, Frank and Lisa drove hundreds of miles north and began seminary, specifically with missions on their minds. After a year of intense preparation, they launched their new careers.

Rather than shuttling off to some corporate hot spot on the coast, they caught a daylong plane ride and took up quarters among the poor in a faraway country that can't be mentioned by name. It's a country that's hostile to all things American. Instead of chatting about stock dividends and fiscal fitness over power lunches with business associates, they chose instead to practice a strange new language in torrid street markets, secret worship services, and ramshackle buses that roar down narrow dirt streets. As empty nesters, Frank and Lisa have leveraged their newfound freedom to connect a strange part of the world to the love of Christ.

Of course, you don't have to cross the ocean to find kingdom work. You might not even have to leave your home. Kingdom work is everywhere. As an empty nester, you may need to invite an elderly parent into your home, or you might be called on to support parents financially and emotionally, as I (Robert) did when my mom was alone and ill late in life. Sure, it was hard at times. To serve my mother in this way was both a privilege and a Christian mandate for Sherard and me (1 Tim. 5:4). And

---

Married Empty Nester
WISE STEPS

- Build new ways of connecting with your husband and enjoying life together.
- Reinvent your life!
- Invest more time in kingdom work that engages your gifts and interests.
- Consider mentoring younger women.

Key Verse: Titus 2:3–5

---

when on a cold Easter morning it fell to me to go into her hospital room and inform her that she had inoperable brain cancer, her words were a vindication of our sacrifices for her. She smiled and said, "Robert, I want you to know how good my life has been these last two years with you and Sherard watching out for me. Thank you."

It's not only elderly parents you can look after and care for in this season of life. Scripture says you are also uniquely positioned to look after the younger women around you who desperately need your wisdom and experience. In this way you can continue to "multiply." Titus 2:4–5 exhorts older women to help younger women learn how to live *smart*. "Encourage the young women to love their husbands, to love their children, to be sensible, pure, workers at home, kind, being subject to their own husbands, so that the word of God will not be dishonored." Every new generation of women needs to hear that. It's a challenging message that's best heard from the lips of older women whose life experiences (both good and bad) confirm such wisdom. In this season of life, you can do that!

Several years after a painful divorce, Shirley James was asked by one of the pastors at our (Robert's) church to mentor a young woman. Shirley was skeptical. "I weighed his request against the amount of credibility I thought I had, and it seemed I fell short." But with the encouragement of friends, Shirley took a leap of faith and met a discouraged young woman named Jennifer for lunch.

"We ate and chatted for a while. She told me about her troubled childhood, and I told her about my divorce. As we wrapped up, I felt I needed to be clear about my concerns. I said, 'Well, now you know my story. My marriage failed, and I've got some wounds. Can you really be interested in taking me on as your mentor?' Of course, I expected her to say no. I had prepared for it all week. It was the sort of self-rejection I was used to by now. But then to my amazement Jennifer said yes! When I asked her why she would choose me, she said, 'I feel I can trust you because of your scars. You've been hurt, and you've felt unworthy just as I have, so I know you'll be real with me.'"

Looking back now, Shirley sees that this was when her life really started to turn back in the direction it was always meant to take. "For the first time I began to see that my pain, which I thought was a mark of my failure and uselessness, could actually be used by God to bless others."

Shirley met with Jennifer weekly, talking through the pain, disappointment, and fear each of them had experienced and finding hope in God's promises and principles. Each time they met, Shirley realized more and more that God was healing both of them in the process. In the years that followed, Shirley had the privilege of giving Jennifer away at her wedding and becoming a grandmother (called Nonie) to Jennifer's little girl, Sophie.

Shirley's daughters have now all grown up to be mature Christian women—women who have learned a lot from their mother. Meanwhile, Shirley is still being fruitful and multiplying by actively pursuing other young women who are interested in spiritually intimate, honest relationships. Mentoring is a great way to invest your life and advance God's kingdom.

Married with In-Laws and Grandchildren

In this season your family has expanded. And with that expansion you have been given new roles and new responsibilities. There are also new rules to play by.

Some women really struggle here. They have trouble adjusting to the "strangers" their children bring home as mates as well as the new values, new ways of doing things, new schedules, and new identities that come with them. Maybe your daughter has picked up new interests you care little for. Maybe she's going to spend this Christmas with her husband's family and not, as she's always done, with you. Or maybe your son's politics have shifted away from yours. In these situations, it's easy to criticize, control, demand, or intrude without even realizing it.

Be careful here. It's important to start right and stay right. This is the time, after all, when your *child* must focus on "leaving and cleaving" with their new spouse. So for you, this is the time for establishing new, healthy boundaries between you and your children's marriages and for building strong, accepting relationships with their spouses. For instance, it blesses a son when *you* reach out to the young woman he's chosen to spend his life with and genuinely embrace her. Best of all is when you present an attitude that says, "How can I support, help, and bless you?" (1 Pet. 3:8–11).

Your grandparent role is vital too. Unfortunately, I (Robert) never had the opportunity to connect with my grandparents when I was growing up. All but one of them had died by the time I was old enough to be aware of them, and the surviving one, Granny, was a bedridden invalid. So I missed out on experiencing the powerful role my grandparents could play.

Married with In-Laws and Grandchildren
WISE STEPS

- ☞ Make the most of your role as a grandparent.
- ☞ Continue your kingdom work. Invest in young people.
- ☞ Deepen your friendships and make new ones.
- ☞ Find ways to be God's light in the world.

Key Verse: 1 Peter 3:8–11; 2 Timothy 1:5

My kids were much more blessed. They had grandparents who both loved them and were involved in their lives. And what a difference that made! Their presence has given my children a greater sense of connectedness, shared values, heritage, and legacy, not to mention a bigger perspective on life.

So as a grandmother, your work on your family's behalf is not finished. In new and refreshing ways you can make your life count for your grandchildren's betterment. Slip them a dose of wisdom every chance you get. Wrap it in holiday cakes, birthday cards, and warm words. Be a model of love and encouragement. Tell your grandchildren stories of your life. I will always treasure the memories of my mom mesmerizing my children with tales of growing up in a small Louisiana town: her rides on her pony, Buttermilk; digging up arrowheads in her backyard; her Jewish friends who opened her eyes to the larger world; and the account of Charles Lindbergh landing his plane in a bean field near her home. In everything show your grandchildren how life can finish with strength and dignity. In doing so, you will leave your mark on the next generation.

You can mentor people outside your family too. Remember, you were designed for this (Titus 2:3–5; 2 Tim. 2:2). And by this phase of life, you should be well armed with both spiritual wisdom and countless life experiences that add wit and insight to your outlook for helping younger people better live their lives. And, as in all other seasons of life, find ways to shine your light in the world. Volunteer with a nonprofit, go on a short-term (or even long-term!) mission trip, find a cause you're passionate about—such as sex trafficking, the African AIDS epidemic, or breast cancer—and be a champion for that cause. It is amazing what God can accomplish through you in a season when you have the maturity to care less about who gets the credit than about seeing God's kingdom purposes advance in the best way possible.

Late-in-Life Widow

"A single person is missing for you, and the whole world is empty."[1] These are the words Philippe Ariès used to describe the grief and displacement that follow the death of a loved one. It's an emptiness we are all

Late-in-Life Widow
WISE STEPS

- ☞ Serve others.
- ☞ Mentor younger women.
- ☞ Do kingdom work.

Key Verse: 1 Timothy 5:10

destined to feel at some time or another, but among the living it is most often women who are robbed of the closest presence of all: that of a spouse. While only 7 percent of men age sixty-five and over are widowers, over a third of women in this age group are widows.[2]

Novelist Joan Didion is one such woman. As Ariès would say, Didion's world emptied shortly after Christmas 2003 when her husband, author John Gregory Dunne, died of heart seizure at the dinner table. Didion came home from the emergency room and tried to carry on as before.

The problem is, she kept trying to carry on *exactly* as before, as if John were due to arrive momentarily. She left his desk untouched. Open books remained so, ready for John's probing eye. His clothes and shoes were kept in place. He was coming home. It took Didion months to see the absurdity of her actions. She had forsaken the future for the past, something that's easy to do in this season of life.[3]

God cares for widows, and the Bible accordingly has a lot to say about them. Indeed, much of 1 Timothy 5 is specifically devoted to discussing the subject of older and younger widows. Younger widows, according to the apostle Paul's instruction, should seek to reenter married life (1 Tim. 5:14–15). Their mind-set needs to be more "single" than "widow." That means dating again, focusing on a career, and preparing for marriage again, possibly even new children. Paul's message is clear: God wants younger widows to reengage in mainstream life as much as possible rather than languish as untimely victims.

Older widows (those over sixty years old, according to Paul; 1 Tim. 5:9) will have a different rhythm. Life's opportunities have narrowed. It's not that remarriage is out of the question. It's not. And it's wonderful when it happens. But for many, remarriage is not realistic. There are many other good things to live for: grandchildren, friends, serving others, various kinds of kingdom work, mentoring, and prayer, to name a few. If these things have already been a meaningful part of your life, then these cultivated habits of the heart are not hard to expand on. If not, now is the time to expand your life.

The real oxygen of life is in giving. Nowhere is that better seen than in the last seasons of life. Selfishness doesn't work here. Nothing is more pitiful than a demanding, self-absorbed, grasping elderly person. On the other hand, few things are more radiant and vibrant than a loving, other-centered, grace-filled senior. Jesus was right. It is "more blessed to give than to receive" (Acts 20:35). And nowhere is that truth illustrated more clearly than in the way people look and act as earthly life is wrapping up.

For more than twenty-five years I (Robert) have watched young people fill the home of Kitty Longstreth, a longtime widow. I have met few people as alive as Kitty. Now eighty-five, she has devoted her "alone years" to encouraging, praying for, and serving others. Many people in our community would say they owe their spiritual lives to Kitty. Almost any hour of the day, a young woman is at Kitty's house, where she is pointed to God. And as much as Kitty has blessed others, this posture of giving and loving has made her own life equally rich and meaningful.

So don't waste your life looking back as an older widow. Focus instead on the good you can yet do in life. Devote yourself to others. Love. Mentor. Befriend the friendless. Show the strength of a woman who believes God's promises and works to see their fulfillment in her life.

Glorified Saint

On the earth you made only the barest beginning to your life. You knew it. Your heart told you so. Your Bible said it, too. You believed your greatest adventures and your best joys were being reserved for this last season of your life.

And now you're here!

You are in eternity; your beautiful personality, gifts, interests, relationships—all living in a heavenly, "glorified" body! And what a place to live! Heaven is better than you could have ever imagined. There are surprises everywhere. But before you plunge into them, there is a powerful meeting you must have with God—one on One—to sum up the life you lived on earth. This should not come as a surprise. You were told throughout your life this moment would arrive. God spoke of it in His Word: "For we must all appear before the judgment seat of Christ, so that each one of us may be recompensed for his deeds in the body, according to what he has done, whether good or bad" (2 Cor. 5:10).

Everything will be clear in this moment of infallible evaluation. Everything you did in your earthly life—as God's feminine image bearer—will be taken into account by the God who never forgets. For your acts of courageous faith and obedience, you will receive a reward that will awe and humble you (1 Cor. 3:10–14). For faithlessness and worldly compromise, your loss of reward will hurt (v. 15).

God will also give you new responsibilities and new treasures in heaven. Exactly what those are will be based on how well you followed Christ and God's Word while on earth (Matt. 19:27–30; 25:14–29). This is the clear teaching of Scripture (Matt. 6:20; Luke 12:33; 1 Tim. 6:18–19).

Wisdom Is Now Vindicated

- ❧ Your wise moves on earth are rewarded by God in heaven.
- ❧ Your life is praised and commended by God.
- ❧ You are entrusted with new responsibilities and new adventures in God's eternal kingdom based on your earthly faithfulness to Him and His Word.

Key Verse: 2 Corinthians 5:10; Matthew 25:14–30

For sure you are *in* heaven by the grace of God alone (Eph. 2:8–9). But it is equally true that your experience, standing, and life in heaven will be shaped by the kind of life you lived while on earth.

So choose wisely before you reach this final season of life. Live a reward-winning lifestyle so that you can walk away from your coming appointment with God with His praise and commendation ringing in your ears (Matt. 25:21) as you step into a heavenly life of unimaginable rewards. No, you won't live a perfect life on earth. No one does that. You will know failure, compromise, and shame at times. But cling to faith. Repent from periodic bouts with unbelief and worldliness. And when you finish this life, finish as one who trusted God and was blessed by Him. Live this kind of life, and you'll find that one of God's greatest delights is in giving you and others eternal rewards in heaven.

Every godly woman will find the same reality as she enters this final, glorious season of life. Faith pays off. Not only did faith reward her with the best of an earthly life (which she now understands far better), but it has now rewarded her with a rich heavenly life too. This promise is what every godly woman should hold on to and treasure in her heart.

The Reality of Different Seasons

In today's world it is likely that for every woman who sees herself as fitting in to the "standard" progress of the seasons, there is another who doesn't. These are the exceptions that are, in fact, the rule for many millions of women.

Maybe that is you. Maybe for you life doesn't fit these general seasons of life we have described at all. Perhaps that is because of circumstances you could not control, or perhaps it is because of difficulties you helped create. But regardless of the reason, your life has taken a different course than you expected.

My (Robert's) good friend Sandy Bone is one who knows that the expected seasons of life can sometimes get off track. Early in her fifties Sandy had her life turned upside down. After twenty-six years of marriage and raising two children, Sandy's husband was tragically killed in an automobile accident. Suddenly the flow of life Sandy had long experienced made a hard U-turn into an unexpected new life: single again. Thrown into this strange new season, Sandy needed a game plan. The path that once seemed straight and simple was now crowded with new forks and bends.

Tragedy can do that. It can rip you from your comfort zone and set you down hard in a place where you're not sure what to do next. Divorce can do this too. So can infertility, remaining unmarried, marrying a man who already has kids, or being a single mom. In these and other cases, the more typical and sequential seasons of life get scrambled, rearranged, or even repeated. So what do you do? How do you find your footing, make wise moves, and fulfill your Core Callings when the scenery of your life takes on an out-of-the-ordinary color?

You can start the process of discovering your new ground rules by blending two or more of the common seasons of life into a new, hybrid category that best describes your individual situation. First, select from the ten seasons the ones that best describe your life now. For instance, if you have three grade-school children but are recently divorced, then the two seasons that best align themselves with where you are now would be "Single" and "Married with Grade-Schoolers."

Next, select from these two seasons the wise steps in each that best apply to your particular situation. By combining these steps, you will find wisdom and direction for your new, hybrid season: "Single with Grade-Schoolers."

You can do this with any exception to the ten standard seasons. Did you marry a man with young-adult children? Then you are "Newly Married with Young-Adult Children." Are you a young mom who just got engaged? Then you are "Single and Engaged with Preschoolers." If you're an older single woman, you can choose steps from "Single," "Empty Nester," and "Late-in-Life Widow." The point is, by blending any of the more common seasons of life, you can create a wise course for your life. If you are in a hybrid season of life, take a moment to create your own "wise moves" in the box on the next page.

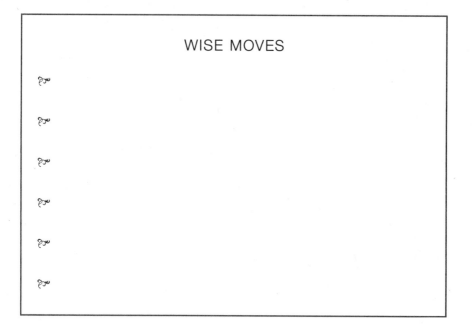

Blending the seasons and figuring out her wise moves is what Sandy had to do. The tragic car accident converted her from a "Married Empty Nester" to a "Single Empty Nester." Like most single people, she needed a job. But which? Sandy had a college degree in teaching, but she hadn't used those skills except for a brief time when she led the women's ministry at our church. The idea of having to support herself was terrifying. Initially she opened her home to international students to help offset the rent and utilities. She also worked at Dillards for $8.50 an hour. As humbling as this was, Sandy knew it was God's way of stretching her character in new and unexpected ways. "This is what I had to keep telling myself," she says with a smile. In this kind of situation, a woman must choose between faith and despair. Sandy chose faith.

Through it all Sandy's Christian friends were a great source of encouragement. "I couldn't have made it without them. They were incredible." Her adult children offered their support too, but they could go only so far. They needed their space and the opportunity to live their own lives. Just because Sandy was single again did not mean she could use her situation to bond with them in the exact same way she had before. Sandy understood this, but it also meant she felt really alone.

After a year of merely making ends meet, Sandy knew it was time to do something more meaningful with her life. As we discussed earlier, singles need to focus on ability and career development, while empty nesters need new work after kids in which to invest their lives. Being both single and an empty nester, Sandy began to investigate where her skills and interests could best be used. One thing kept surfacing: she liked to help people who were hurting. This realization led her to take "the wildest, riskiest leap of my life."

She enrolled in graduate school to become a professional counselor. "I was older than all my professors and even the dean of the college. I had to work really, really hard. I cried more in my statistics classes than at any other time in my life. But it became more and more evident that God was with me, sustaining me, empowering me. It was amazing what He did for me." We who watched were also amazed—amazed at God and this wonderful woman He was blessing.

At age fifty-eight, after three and one-half years of graduate studies and another three and one-half years of residency work, Sandy took her national boards and became a licensed counselor. Her life and faith heroics set an example for all of us who watched her during those years. And God rewarded her for it too, not only with a good job but also with a new husband! I had the privilege of marrying Gayle and Sandy, and it was probably the most gratifying wedding I have ever performed. Before me was a woman whose bold, courageous faith God had rewarded with a better life. I recently asked Sandy, now sixty-five, how things were going. "I'm at the happiest, most exciting time of my life," she replied. I wasn't a bit surprised.

Sometimes, as with Sandy, life circumstances have scrambled your seasons. And sometimes you realize you ended up scrambling your own seasons with choices that were not, in fact, "wise moves." My (Shaunti's) friend Kim in my core group has been transparent and vulnerable about the choices that led to her being an unmarried mom in her late twenties. She is now in her mid thirties and is in a hybrid season of life ("Single Mother of a Grade-Schooler") that is pretty intense. Many demands. Financial pressures. No one to share the tasks with. Little sleep. Kim adores her son, ·but as she readily shares today, it is accurate that life choices can forever change a life path. God can take *any* human choice and bring something beautiful from it, but it does often come at a high price. It makes so much more sense to take care with life choices whenever those choices rest with you—to avoid, wherever possible, the regrets of fighting the way God has designed the seasons of life and instead maximize the opportunities that God presents over our lives as a whole.

Working with the Seasons of Life: Four Principles

So now that you know what the seasons of life are, what are *you* supposed to do with them? As you have progressed through these last two chapters, you probably already have gotten a sense for the answer to that. So let's summarize four principles for working with the seasons of life, based on the compass of God's Word, that will help you determine how to manage *your* life in *your* season.

There Is a Time for Everything

First, as you have seen, God has given you a unique design and callings, and He has appointed the time for you to fulfill each of them . . . and it won't be all at once. To paraphrase Ecclesiastes, there will be one point when you are to build up and another when you are to tear down. There will be a point at which you are going to plant certain gifts and a time when you are to harvest the fruit from those gifts.

Your Core Callings Never Go Away

The second principle is that your Core Callings never go away. But each season of life naturally lends itself to a *different* way of fulfilling them. For example, everyone has the same calling to advance the next generation. But someone who is a parent of children at home has those opportunities in their face every day and will naturally have opportunities to focus on that calling. By contrast, a single woman or an empty nester or a late-in-life widow who does not have children at home has the same calling to be fruitful and multiply. But she will have to *look* for those opportunities, and what she does will often look different simply because she probably has more time to pour life into these young lives.

For example, our church has a dynamite Explorer Girls group for grade-school girls one night a week when the girls have fellowship and are challenged to build their lives according to God's plan. That group is entirely led by a thirty-something-year-old single woman who is a Ph.D. scientist and is very busy . . . but who recognizes that since she is not married and has a bit more freedom to make her own choices for her schedule, this is a time when she can really invest herself in these girls. So she is being purposeful about pouring her life into this group and is fulfilling her "be fruitful and multiply" calling in a totally different way than she might when she has children at home.

A Choice for One Thing Is a Choice against Another

Third, in each season of life, a choice *for* something is a choice *against* something else. In his book *Choosing to Cheat*, pastor Andy Stanley talks about this. He says that every day we are making choices—whether we think about it that way or not—and we are going to cheat *something*. As he summarizes the message, "There is not enough time to get it all done. Somebody is going to feel left out, neglected, or cheated. So the real question is not *are* you cheating, but *who* are you cheating? You need to be intentional about the choice."[4]

Instinctively we know this is true. With limited time, every hour we spend on one thing is an hour that we will not have to spend on something else. Anyone who has a husband or boyfriend who works long hours understands this at the most fundamental level. If your husband leaves the house at 7:30 in the morning and walks back in the door at 7:00 every evening, you have a limited window to see him and spend time with him. But suppose golf is important to him, and he spends four hours every Saturday morning with friends on the golf course. You can be glad he's having fun but still feel cheated. You have these precious few hours when he's not at work, and you instinctively feel that the choice he's made *for* golf is a choice *against* you and the kids.

But the thing is: we *all* do the same thing. For example, every hour you spend cleaning up after dinner and putting the house in order after the kids are in bed is an hour you aren't spending cuddling with your husband on the sofa watching television. If you are single, in a high-powered career, every business trip you accept that takes you away from the weekly singles Bible study at church is one more night when you aren't having an opportunity to meet Christian men as friends—and maybe something more later on.

Is either choice wrong or right? Not necessarily. However, you can look to your current season of life to help you understand which choice you should make, which leads to the final principle.

Make Choices Appropriate to Your Season

Our fourth principle is that in order to live according to God's best for you now, you must understand what season you are in and purposefully make the appropriate lifestyle choices to go with it.

With every Faith Step we will come to a point where the rubber meets the road, and for this second step of embracing a big-picture understanding of life, it's right here. At some point we have to move beyond principle and actually change our choices, if changes are indeed needed to live according to the season we are in.

Suppose, for instance, you had made the purposeful choice to step *away* from a career for a time to stay home with small children. But now the years have passed and the kids are in high school or leaving home, and you realize they don't need you every moment. So this may be a time to take a deep breath, pray for courage, and fully jump into using certain "subdue and rule" gifts in ways you had put on the back burner in previous seasons of life.

In my (Shaunti's) core group, Debbie is in that exact situation. She was a stay-at-home mom, but as her kids went into school, she became a teacher so her schedule matched theirs. But now her third child is about to graduate from high school. She has made a great deal of kingdom impact in all the children she has taught over the years. But now she's recognizing that once she is in that empty-nester season of life, she may have some completely different opportunities for "subdue and rule" impact that wouldn't have "fit" before. During her summers off school, for example, she realizes—wow, she could really think outside the box! She could do a monthlong missions trip to build orphanages in a developing country, for example! She would *never* have been able to do that when her children were living at home, but now she can.

Once you start purposefully thinking of things this way, it is so much simpler to understand what your decision should be when you are presented with competing choices.

Up until now, we've been talking about really big-picture choices like, for singles, "Make sure you don't work so much you don't have time to go on dates." But like all the other Faith Steps, embracing a big-picture perspective of life and living according to the seasons of life can help you check even your most simple day-to-day choices against the standard of God's Word, too.

I (Shaunti) had a chance to do this recently. At the end of this past winter, I was in Colorado Springs for two days doing some broadcast recording, and a blizzard sprang up and threatened to prevent me from flying out on a Friday afternoon. They were quickly expecting two *feet* of snow.

One of my publishers is in Colorado Springs, and one of my friends at the publisher said, "You know all flights will be shut down tomorrow. The airline will be trying to take volunteers to delay and fly out Sunday. If you'd like to do that, call me and we'll go skiing in the mountains tomorrow." I was *dying* to do that. I absolutely love skiing, and I rarely get to do it. I would miss the kids' soccer games on Saturday back in Atlanta . . . but there would be *ten* soccer games and only *one* chance to go skiing on two feet of fresh snow!

But then I literally thought about this Faith Step and the need to use the Core Callings to help us evaluate our choices—even those small ones. I had to follow this step of living according to my season of life. My choice might have been different and I might have decided to take a day to go skiing if I was a stay-at-home mom and already doing a great job of "being fruitful and multiplying." But instead, as you know, that is something I need to work on. So I told my friend, "Thanks for the offer, but I'll have to take you up on that in about ten years."

I headed for the airport, didn't volunteer to be bumped to a different flight, and did get home so I could see my kids' soccer games. What was most important was letting them know that Mommy cared *most* about being with them. It really helped to have that choice put clearly in the context of how my season of life impacted my Core Callings.

Remember, even if life doesn't quite look like this for you—if life has thrown you curveballs, perhaps—you can still prioritize the Core Callings and reach out to others. And anyone who *hasn't* had as many curveballs has a kingdom opportunity to be there for someone who has.

For example, my friend Kim, the single mom I mentioned, *has* to work, no matter how much she might prefer to be a stay-at-home mom and focus on her son. And the rest of us have to consider the responsibility we might have here. James 1:27 says, "Pure and undefiled religion in the sight of our God and Father is this: to visit orphans and widows in their distress, and to keep oneself unstained by the world."

I view single moms or dads and their children as today's version of "orphans and widows." They are weary and would love some help or just a break. As we focus on our season of life, we must be purposeful about ministering to those whose seasons of life might have gotten scrambled. For example, my son and Kim's son have been best friends since preschool. If I'm trying to fulfill my "be fruitful and multiply" calling, need to force myself away from my computer, and am picking up my kids from school anyway, . . . why can't I also pick up Kim's son from his school for a play-date and give Kim a break?

As you can see by now, it is all a matter of thinking about these things, evaluating how you are spending your time, being purposeful about making the right choices for your current season of life and preparing well for the next one. You can start by using the box on this page to capture anything you feel you need to change, in order to live according to your season of life.

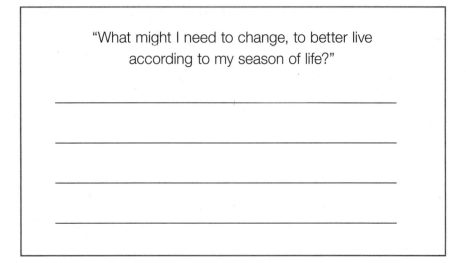

As we move forward, one factor that we haven't talked about yet affects much of what we've been discussing. I (Shaunti) have seen that it is, for many of us, a major factor that impacts a huge amount of what we do and how well placed we are to fulfill our Core Callings. Indeed, this one factor requires taking a Faith Step that often affects everything else and determines how easy or hard it is to actually take all the other Faith Steps toward God's best for our lives.

I'm talking about *me*, and have to address this subject before we can move any further; we'll tackle it in the next chapter.

9

Using Wisdom with a Man

They were on their way to a wedding. It would be a lavish affair, so Carolyn had to have exactly the right dress. She knew from experience that the photographers—there would be at least a dozen—would be as apt to shoot her as the bride, but the last thing she wanted to do was steal the show. After hours of searching the racks at Saks Fifth Avenue, she found what she wanted. As she left the store, Carolyn was surprised to see that the sun had already ducked well below the western edge of the cityscape. It was getting late.

Across town, John Kennedy Jr. noticed the time too. He picked up his sister-in-law, Lauren, and headed for the municipal airport as quickly as he could. But traffic was bad. So were the gawkers. Pedestrians, street vendors, and other drivers—they all craned their necks to get a look at John in his shiny white convertible. Traffic crawled.

By the time John and Lauren met Carolyn at the hangar, night was beginning to fall. John scrambled to get his small plane ready for takeoff. He had been flying for a few years but was not yet instrument rated. He was licensed to pilot a plane only when visual conditions were good, not into a darkening night, not into haze.

One of his flying instructors, uncomfortable with the situation, offered to accompany John on the flight to Martha's Vineyard, but John turned him down, saying he "wanted to do it alone." After all, he had flown at least 35 trips to or from Martha's Vineyard, including several at night. He figured he could fly at night by experience, common sense and instinct, even if not by instruments alone.[1]

At twelve minutes after sundown, John roared down the runway in his Piper Saratoga. Carolyn and her sister chatted behind him. Moments after being airborne, a thick haze developed, veiling the sky. John struggled to see his way. He aimed his plane out over the ocean toward Martha's Vineyard. But as time went on and conditions worsened, John lost all his bearings. Up and down, water and sky—they looked the same. "You can be upside down and turning to the left and your body is telling you you're right side up and turning right," pilot Edward Francis later said of such conditions.[2] Every instrument-rated pilot learns to rely solely on his or her instruments rather than on what they feel is right at the time, but John wasn't able to do that.

As Carolyn huddled with her sister, hoping for the best, John made a decision. Supposing that he was dangerously close to the water, he yanked the yoke toward his lap to gain altitude. His instruments told him not to do that—that his wings weren't level—but John didn't notice. Suddenly the Piper plunged seaward, caught in the grip of a violent corkscrew dive it never escaped.

Compass-Guided Living

John Kennedy Jr. lost his way and then his life because he decided to fly on nothing but his instincts and feelings. Unfortunately, those failed him. And today they are failing many people who may not realize that they, too, are essentially trying to guess their way through life. As we said early in this book, the view today is clouded by new choices, new opportunities, and new conflicts. If we try flying blind, it can be deadly.

Instead, as you now know, compass-guided womanhood means managing ourselves by bold faith in God and His Word. It means refusing to trust our senses and feelings, especially since those can all too easily get turned around by worldly pressures and options. Instead, we must place absolute trust in and base our choices solely on our equivalent of an aircraft's instrument panel—the compass of God's Word.

Compass-guided womanhood is important in every area of life, but there are few areas in which it is as day-to-day life changing as when relating with (and choosing) a man. Instinct alone in this area can be especially deadly. Feelings can be deceiving, regardless of whether one is a single looking around or has been married fifty years. We've all been led down the wrong path in this area at times. And, further, even the most sold-out woman of God may have absorbed the world's inaccurate and damaging information about men without realizing it and thus may unintentionally be relating to men in a way that leads to a downward spiral instead of a smooth flight.

Faith Step #3: Use Wisdom with a Man

Forcing ourselves to trust God's compass with men—and act based on what it tells us—will lead us to use wisdom with a man. Conversely, ignoring that compass can make our relationships with men much more difficult.

The Ramifications for Our Core Callings

The ramifications of this one Faith Step are huge. Whether we use wisdom with a man (especially a husband) often affects every aspect of our lives, including our ability to live out our Core Callings. Let's look at how.

LEAVE AND CLEAVE

First, obviously, whether we use wisdom with men affects our calling to "leave and cleave." Those of us who are married or engaged obviously need daily wisdom in our relationships with our husbands or fiancés. And for single women, understanding men and using wisdom with them is absolutely critical since it often affects their ability not just to "find a man" but to find the *right* man—and thus affects nearly everything about the rest of their lives. That said, as every older single knows, using wisdom is no guarantee of finding Prince Charming and living happily ever after.

I also know some single women who have been so hurt by men that they shut off their heart and say, "I don't need a man!" For them, using wisdom with a man includes working to move past the bitterness, forgive where necessary, and being careful about future choices, so their calling (and underground desire) to "leave and cleave" is not held hostage to old hurts.

But I also know many wonderful single women in their thirties and forties—such as my thirty-nine-year-old friend Angie in my core group—who are in the opposite situation. They have a hole in their heart because they are trusting God and being careful and wise with men . . . and still have not yet been brought the opportunity to cleave with a godly husband.

If that is you, we want you to hear us when we say this: that "hole in the heart" feeling is legitimate. Yes, God's grace is sufficient for those who are lonely; yes, we can learn to be content in all situations; and yes, all of us need to look to Jesus (not a man) to complete us fully. But that doesn't necessarily cure the loneliness that comes when you are missing the companionship that every human being is built for. For you, the key to "using wisdom with a man" in this waiting time is to make it a time of "active waiting." As we said in the "seasons of life" discussion, learn about how God has actually wired men—what they need, find appealing, and are turned off by— instead of basing your ideas on guesswork, magazines, media, and assumptions. Don't let your understandable feelings of long-ing pull you away from following your biblical compass. And unless God has given you direction otherwise (which does sometimes happen), if you are not currently in a situation where you can meet new men and develop healthy friendships with them, evaluate whether you need to take further steps in that area. Unless you are one of the few women who are called to lifelong singleness, all this will prepare you to "leave and cleave" well in the future.

BE FRUITFUL AND MULTIPLY

Whether we use wisdom with men clearly affects our ability to live out this Core Calling as well. Whether or not you are bonded to a godly man and work to keep your relationship strong will impact your ability to bring children into the world (or adopt the parentless) and raise them in a home that is firm and united in the goal of launching godly children into the world.

Now, notice I said "impact" your ability. It is not the end of the story. If you, for example, are married to a man who is not a follower of Christ, it is not that that you will be unable to raise your children to love the Lord and launch them well. Of course not! My friend Wendy in my core group married her Jewish husband during a few years in her twenties when she was not walking with the Lord. He is a wonderful man, and we will never stop praying for him, and in the meantime their two children have grown up to be adults who love Jesus—but that's been despite the fact that only one parent had that goal. Yet how much better would it have been (and how much heartbreak could have been avoided) if Wendy and her husband had been united in a Christian "be fruitful and multiply" focus.

In a similar way, you may have used wisdom all along the way and still find yourself struggling due to events not of your choosing. Do you remember, in chapter 5, my describing Susan, my best friend growing up, who for years has been a homeschooling mom to five children? Well today she also finds herself a single mother to those five children because her husband suddenly left her for another woman. She used wisdom and still found herself in a heartbreaking situation. So her version of "using wisdom with a man" is suddenly different: it is to be wise about male friendships today in case (as she says) "there's some godly man out there who is just waiting for a ready-made large family!" And as unnecessary as it might sound in such a clearly lopsided situation, "using wisdom with a man" also includes reflecting on her eighteen years with her husband and any areas she can improve on if God does bring another man into her life. Although her situation is about as close to a truly one-sided case as I've seen, I'm proud of her for recognizing that there are always things we can improve on and for her willingness to work on those areas. She's even made a "full disclosure" list of her weaknesses to show to any serious suitor!

SUBDUE AND RULE

Finally, using wisdom with men also affects how we "subdue and rule" because it makes a big difference in how well we are launched for kingdom work or how distracted we are from it. I have so often heard women say, "When my husband and I are at odds, it's like nothing is right with the world until it's resolved." Conversely, we women know how wonderful it feels to be supported in doing what we are called to do.

Many of us have made choices with men—good and bad—that have had an impact on how well we can step into our calling to subdue and rule. Thankfully, in all these areas, God says He can redeem even the bad choices, and He "causes all things to work together for good to those who love God, to those who are called according to His purpose" (Rom. 8:28). But ideally, it is simply better to think about using wisdom on the front end if we can!

Getting Started

So all that said, what does using wisdom with a man look like? In our experience one of *the* most overlooked factors in using wisdom with a man starts with operating based on correct, biblical information about what men need—rather than flying by instincts that are often wrong simply because women are so very different. As mentioned earlier, I (Shaunti) have spent eight years researching and writing about men's deepest thoughts, feelings, and needs. And of course, Robert has been living in a male brain for a long time! The following is a good summary of what both of us feel it is most important to know as a starting point, and then we hope you will dig into the subject further.

> Using wisdom with a man starts with operating based on correct information about what men need—rather than flying by instincts that are often wrong. ❧

What Drives a Man

Do you know what drives a man? Your man? Any man? It's *performance*. It is actually accomplishing something—

whether that means making his wife happy or landing enough deals that he can pay the mortgage next month. Where women most want to feel special, loved, and valued for who we are on the inside, men most need to feel validated and noticed for what they accomplish on the outside.

In essence, a man's whole sense of personhood and well-being centers on his performance. Michelangelo spoke for all men when he said, "It is only well with me when I have a chisel in my hand." Men are life's ultimate action figures. George Gilder, a keen observer of social science, put it this way: "Manhood at the most basic level can be validated and expressed only in action. . . . Men must perform."[3]

An oil company used to advertise its product with this slogan: "It's performance that counts." That's really the slogan and mind-set of men everywhere. It drives everything men do—and is a huge factor in how they feel about themselves. It's the reason men are reluctant to stop and ask for directions. To do so is to admit, "I haven't performed well. I've failed. I didn't cut it." A college biology teacher once asked his class the following question: "Why, in the reproductive process, does the female offer only one egg while the male offers millions upon millions of sperm?" A woman raised her hand and said, "Because those guys won't ask for directions either." She's probably right. It goes that deep! That's why men would rather drive on, hoping to get it right rather than pull over and ask for help: the sinking sense that they have failed, that they are inadequate (even though we would never see it that way!) is a man's most uncomfortable, even painful, feeling.

In my (Shaunti's) research with men, I was shocked to realize that underneath a man's confident exterior lies a lot of self-doubt. In every area of life, men continually ask themselves, *Did I come through? Do I measure up?* That's a man's basic life question, and believe it or not, we as women play a crucial role in the way he answers it.

In the classic fairy tale *Snow White and the Seven Dwarfs,* a wicked witch repeatedly asks her magic mirror this familiar question: "Mirror, mirror, on the wall, who's the fairest of them all?" Of course, she did not get the answer she wanted. The witch's torment was that the mirror regularly reminded her of her second-class status to Snow White. Eventually, that negative reflection was her undoing.

Men have mirrors too. And these mirrors possess a tremendous power that can either affirm or undo them. Most men have two such mirrors; Christian men have three. As they stand before each of their mirrors, they pose a question similar to that of the witch: "Mirror, mirror, on the wall, am I doing any good at all?" In other words, "Am I doing what inherently matters most to me—performing, delivering, coming through?" If his mirrors affirm him, a man feels good about himself. He powers up. But if these mirrors frown on him and reflect failure, disappointment, and shame, this loss will unleash inside him the same frustration, anger, and humiliation the witch felt. The problem is, this is no fairy tale. This is real life, and what he sees in these mirrors has an impact on more lives than only his own.

So what are these three mirrors? For two-mirrored men, they are the woman in his life and his work. Christian men look into a third mirror as well: the Word of God. Each of these mirrors offers its own unique reflection of a man's daily performance. The workplace mirror reflects the value of a man's skills and his performance in using those skills. The Word of God mirrors something much deeper. It reflects to him the thoughts, secrets, and motivations of his heart (Heb. 4:12).

Then there's the woman in his life. We women are the most personal mirror our men have. In your eyes, face, and responses, your husband, fiancé, or boyfriend receives an evaluation of his life in ways that are deeply important to him. In you he sees and feels his life's worth most intensely. If you are wise, you will often reflect back to your man his best traits and accomplishments. And in tough times, when he's had failures, your reflection of belief in him will help him believe in himself again and not give up.

Positive reflections build up and empower a man. Conversely, show a man his failures daily, and it simply confirms the self-doubt he already felt about himself—a self-doubt that saps his strength and hinders his ability to be his best for you. In some cases his motivation to be the hero is so sapped that he may eventually let his best self go for the dark side. To have his shortcomings rehearsed in his wife's mirror on a consistent basis may cause a man to lose his masculine will altogether. In the harsh glare of criticism, it will whither. The truth is, a man will often become what is reflected back to him. Our mirror is *that* powerful.

Remember, performance and achieving something—which includes your happiness and security!—is what drives a man. So it's important never to take your man's accomplishments or efforts for granted. Celebrate his victories. Even embellish them. In hard times major on the best in him. Encourage him in such moments by expressing your belief in him and his abilities. With that inner self-doubt and insecurity always running in the background, fear of failure often holds a man back from trying—even more so in difficult times (such as unemployment or personal crisis) when the risk of failure is high. That's why your belief in him is so important. It helps him believe in himself and go for it. In a man's world it's performance that counts. "Mirror, mirror, on the wall, am I any good at all?" What are you answering back to your man?

His Key Needs

In 1 Peter 3:7, the apostle gives husbands this command, "You husbands in the same way, live with your wives in an understanding way . . . since she is a woman." What wise advice that is! I (Robert) can tell you that no man "speaks woman" naturally. It's an acquired language. It takes research, investigation, practice, and a big dose of humility to learn it.

But look again at 1 Peter 3:7, and you'll notice something there for women, too. It's found in the words *in the same way*. Though Peter is passionately exhorting men to acquire an understanding of women, "in the same way" reminds us that Peter has just said the same thing to us as women; that is, we need to work to understand men, too, because men and women will always be alien beings to one another.

So for the rest of this chapter, we will be entirely focusing on what women can do to understand men, not the other way around. We can only do what *we* can do—and as we follow the Bible's compass, even when it means making a one-sided choice, we will often find that God uses that one-sided choice to change the entire relationship.

The most fundamental place to begin is by mastering a man's key needs. While there are many male needs that we should be aware of—

which are all too easy to misunderstand or miss completely—several categories are particularly important to cover here:

MEN NEED ADMIRATION AND RESPECT.

In Ephesians 5, Paul spells out the marital responsibilities of husbands and wives. We see that a man's chief assignment is to love his wife. You would assume that Paul would tell women we have the same responsibility toward our husbands, . . . but he doesn't. Why? Because the deepest need of a man in marriage is not to be loved by his wife but to be admired and respected. That's why Paul concludes Ephesians 5 with these words, "The wife must see to it that she respects her husband" (v. 33).

> Every time we praise our men, we're speaking affirmation to their hidden self-doubt, and life into the core of who they are. ෴

What love is to us, respect is to him. In our world "I love you" means everything. Not so for men. So many men have told me (Shaunti), "If I had to, I could go the rest of my life without hearing my wife say that she loves me. There is no way I could go the rest of my life without hearing my wife say, 'I'm so proud of you.'" Those words are the best "I love you" a man can get. And every time we praise our men in this way, we're speaking affirmation, strength, and satisfaction to their hidden self-doubt, and speaking life into the core of who we are, especially when we do it publicly. To say to him, "I'm so proud of you" in front of others . . . well, for a man, it just doesn't get much better than that. Nothing beats being admired.

In today's modern, liberated day, you may privately be thinking what one woman openly said to me (Shaunti) at one of my events: "You've got to be kidding me! We women finally got our independence from male oppression. There's no way I'm going to be an admiration machine in an apron."

Well, first of all—who said anything about an apron? A well-intentioned effort to meet his needs (just as you want him to meet yours) does not somehow mean that you have to fit into a stereotypical, retro gender role. But more importantly, that statement reflects a fear that is based on a complete and utter myth: the notion that by building up his ego he'll overpower and diminish you. The research-supported reality couldn't be more different. Remember, his ego is merely a shell that masks a lot of private self-doubt. When you affirm his real accomplishments, you aren't inflating an already oversize ego. You are, instead, building up the inner man that is privately insecure and giving him the belief that he can indeed be the man he wants to be—for you.

With this male need for respect and the female need for love in mind, reread chapter 4's outline for biblical marriage and God's plan for the "head" and "helper." Suddenly you will see so intimately just how much those roles are designed to ensure that each partner is given what we need most!

A MAN NEEDS OUR SUPPORT IN HIS WORK AND DREAMS.

Daniel Levinson's mammoth research work, *Seasons of a Man's Life,* revealed that the typical man marries a woman who he thinks will nourish his life vision and help him fulfill his life's work. Levinson also found that if a wife fails to do this or loses interest in what her husband does, the marriage relationship eventually becomes troubled. Why? Because men need their wives to stand with them in their work. They need us to identify with, appreciate, and value the work that defines their lives.

This support is particularly important in times of transition or change, when a man is out of work and trying to find a job or thinks his best shot at success is to change jobs or career paths or take some risky shot at a better life. At such times the support of his wife is crucial. No, he doesn't need you mindlessly to submit to his daring ideas. That could wreck you both. On the other hand, he doesn't need you instinctively to react by bringing up the 101 reasons "why not," either. Rather than blind obedience or emotional reactiveness, what he needs is your wisdom, strength, and encouragement to think outside the box. Help him evaluate, but supportively—including not just the negatives but all the positives for him as well. He doesn't need you always to agree with him, but he *does* need you always to believe in him.

According to Levinson's research, a lot of men consider a risky career move in their late twenties or early thirties. That was certainly true for me (Robert). In my first job after seminary, I copastored a church in Tucson, Arizona. I had a wonderful time there serving a great group of people. During my stay the church experienced significant growth; we hired a number of new staff and built a wonderful facility. It was all coming together.

But then I got a call from old college friends back in Little Rock. They had recently started a new church and were renting space in a small private school. My buddies asked me to consider moving to Little Rock to be their pastor. There were no guarantees. The pay was minimal. But my leadership opportunities would be significantly broadened to allow me to try some of the new and unconventional things I had dreamed of doing as a church leader.

I discussed this opportunity with Sherard, who at the time was pregnant with our second child and had just finished decorating our new home. I explained to her that the salary they were offering me would not be enough for us to buy a home in Little Rock. We would have to rent instead. I also told her that this new church had no facilities; it was meeting in a sweatbox of a school gymnasium. "It's a huge risk to go," I said, "but this church has dreams like ours and offers greater opportunity for me to use my leadership gifts."

I will never forget what happened next. Decades later it still has a huge impact on me emotionally. After a brief pause, she looked into my eyes and smiled—smiled!—and said, "Robert, you can do it. Let's go."

And we did. Together. Her support and encouragement gave me the boost I needed to take this flying leap that has now defined my life more than any other. As I write, I have had twenty-five wonderful years at Fellowship Bible Church. I have recently leaped into a new career of writing and filmmaking, and Sherard said, "Go for that, too!" Great things have happened. But it all starts with a supportive wife.

There is one other area in which a man needs a woman's support. It's in the area of dreaming. Men spend a tremendous amount of energy contemplating what else they could do with their lives. They constantly think,

Where is the best place for me? A big asset to them is having a woman they can think out loud with about these things. Understand that this dream talk is often nothing more than merely that: talk. But it is still important to a man. It helps him process and coordinate his life, measure its value as well as its possibilities. A wise woman knows this. She sees the value in being her man's sounding board. Some women, on the other hand, are confused and perplexed by a man's dreaming. It can scare them.

Does your man bounce around from one seemingly random idea to another when he dreams out loud? Does that drive you crazy? Men love to open their hearts to their women and dream about other possibilities . . . that is, if it's safe. If a man's dreaming out loud is met with reactions like "You've got to be kidding," or all the reasons something won't work, he'll shut down. Maybe forever. And that's a loss for everyone. So let your man dream with you. Encourage and support him. Ask probing questions like: "Help me understand; what are your thoughts behind that? What are all the options, and what would be your financial plan for each?" Or you can affirm him by saying, "You could do that, and you would be good at it." Enter his dreams, and he'll love you for it.

Hear us on this: A man is paying you a big compliment when he invites you to dream with him. He is saying, "I trust you with my heart."

A MAN NEEDS A RECREATIONAL COMPANION.

In his excellent book *His Needs, Her Needs,* Willard Harley comments that for a man, "spending recreational time with his wife is second only to sex."[4] In my (Shaunti's) research, I was surprised to find that the vast majority of men wanted romance just like their wives and viewed going out and playing together as very romantic.

So what does that mean? It means that the couple that plays together *stays* together. Like the retiring medical doctor and his wife mentioned in chapter 8 who bought Harleys together, a man feels a deeper level of intimacy and friendship with his wife when she engages him in his recreational passions. We're not suggesting you have to go paintballing, cliff climbing, or stalk and shoot deer in the mountains to satisfy this need if you truly don't want to. (Although personally, I—Shaunti—love playing paintball!) But we are suggesting that you look for active ways to connect. Educate yourself on his favorite sport. Watch it on TV or take a class on it—they are out there. Or do what my (Robert's) wife did. When we first married, Sherard was about as quick to grab the sports page as I was the fashion section, which was *never*. But before long she realized how important sports were to me. The next thing I knew, she was beating me to the sports page. It was a wise move on her part. Best of all, my wife has become an avid, educated sports fan, and we're both loving every minute of it . . . together!

A MAN NEEDS PHYSICAL RESPONSIVENESS (AND FOR HER TO CARE ENOUGH TO TAKE CARE OF HERSELF).

Some years ago I (Robert) happened to see that a woman's magazine had conducted a survey listing men's and women's favorite leisure activities. I don't remember what the magazine was, or what most of the other numbers were, but I sure remember the top results. The survey reported that the number-one leisure activity for men is sex. No surprise there. But the number-one leisure activity for women was reading! Sex was buried way down the list next to sewing. That difference in interests can lead to some tense moments (or even months or years) in a marriage.

Men are extremely physical, visual creatures—with a physical need that is inextricably tied up with a powerful emotional one. And depending on who you are as a woman—single or married—you must approach this male need carefully.

If you are single, you must draw physical boundaries with your man. In this sexually aware and active world, that is hard to do. It may seem prudish. Early Christians probably felt the same way because immorality was everywhere in the Roman Empire. Contemporary Roman commentators described adultery as a common, everyday behavior. "Pure women," sang Ovid, "are only those who have not been asked."[5] But for us, it is the Core Callings and God's standards, not the moral conditions of a particular culture at a particular time, that shape our choices.

And we have to realize that God's standards are not arbitrary: there is a reason for them. In researching teenagers and single young men and

women, I (Shaunti) was hugely impacted to see the powerful but unintended emotional consequences that arose when a couple had had sex
outside of a marriage commitment: two-thirds of the guys said they would
start to doubt that they could trust their girlfriend, and eight in ten girls
started to worry about losing their boyfriend and (as a result) struggled
with possessive, clingy feelings and behavior. Neither partner wanted those
feelings, but they were sparked because subconsciously each person knew
that they *didn't* have a lifetime marriage commitment.[6] A single Christian
woman will be wise to draw physical boundaries with a man.

For married women, sexual restraint is not the issue. Sexual fulfillment
is. As wives we have an important calling to fulfill a deep need of our
husbands in this area—needs which are not the physical "demands" some
might think but are deeply emotional.
The importance of physical intimacy
to a man is actually about his need to
feel that his wife *desires* him. If a man
feels that his wife desires him, it gives
him a sense of confidence and a sense of
well-being in every other area of his life.
Conversely, if he doesn't feel desired,
it gives him almost a sense of depres-
sion and a lack of well-being in every other area of his life. This probably
explains why God says husbands and wives must not hold back intimacy
from each other. In fact, in 1 Corinthians 7, Paul said that a wife must
fulfill her (sexual) duty to her husband (v. 3), just as a husband must for
his wife.

> If a man feels that his
> wife desires him, it gives
> him a sense of confi-
> dence and a sense of
> well-being in every other
> area of his life. ☙

The word *duty* may sound a bit strong or even oppressive, but Paul
used it to make sure a wife understands how absolutely vital her sexual
responsiveness is to her husband. Willard Harley wrote, "When a man
chooses a wife, he promises to remain faithful to her for life. He makes
this commitment because he trusts her to be as sexually interested in him
as he is in her. . . . Unfortunately in many marriages, the man finds putting his trust in this woman has turned into one of the biggest mistakes of
his life. He has agreed to limit his sexual experience to a wife who is

unwilling to meet that vital need."[7] Why is that? So often we as wives simply do not recognize the importance and centrality of this emotional need to our husbands, and we have never seriously considered it as just as much of a biblical instruction as lifelong fidelity is. Thankfully, once our eyes are opened to this need—and we meet it—we will see that one of *the main reasons* God gives us this instruction is because this particular type of affirmation both empowers a man out in the world and softens him toward his wife, to be the loving and caring man she most longs for!

What sexually fulfills a husband the most? It's *his wife's* satisfaction that satisfies him the most. When your husband knows he has performed in a way that succeeds with you and gives you pleasure, life could not be better. This is a huge emotional longing behind your husband's sexual drive.

Many women assume what her husband wants most is to please himself. Nothing could be further from the truth! I (Robert) have asked thousands of husbands what gives them the greatest sexual pleasure in their marriages. Almost universally they tell me their deepest fulfillment is not in what they get but in how well they please their wives. It's that performance-that-counts thing again.

So sexual fulfillment for a husband is directly related to his wife's enjoyment. A husband loves it when he knows his wife really enjoys their intimacy by the way she responds to him and compliments him. When that happens, a man feels like a *man*—a real man. Her affirmation in this way salves his deep inner self-doubt and gives him the emotional gusto to be the man she needs in every other area of life.

Another area of physical fulfillment and attraction is awkward to talk about but is important to cover here because it is rife with misunderstanding, but it has a big impact. Both single and married women will also be wise to realize that from a neurological standpoint, men's emotions are powerfully tied up with how visually they process the world. I (Robert) can tell you that men absolutely do not expect the supermodel bodies you women *think* we want. We wish you all would just throw all the *Cosmo* magazines away and believe us when we say that that is not what we are looking for. But that said, I (Shaunti) can tell you that, clinically, the male brain is wired (unlike the female brain) so that a man generally will not be romantically, emotionally attracted to a woman unless he is also visually, physically attracted to her. And that usually means that he has to see her making an effort to take care of herself.

Frankly, whether we make an effort to take care of ourselves sends a specific visual signal to a man that we often are completely unaware of. For singles, the visual signal is, "I care about myself enough to take care of myself"; that self-respect is attractive to men, where the reverse is not (in fact, it is often a deal-breaker because he simply *cannot* see her in a romantic way). And for married women, the emotionally important visual signal is, "I care about *you,* my husband, enough, to take care of myself for you." And this signal lasts a lifetime: making a reasonable effort to be healthy (including *not* starving yourself or beginning an unhealthy mental obsession with how you look!), eating well, and staying active enough to go out and do things together is as important at age seventy-five as at twenty-five.

Admiration and respect, support for work and dreams, recreational companionship, and physical responsiveness and care—being wise in these four areas with men will be powerfully effective for any woman.

Some Specifics for Singles

Some of you are thinking, *But I'm not married or engaged. I'm not even seriously dating. What about me?* As we've said earlier, perhaps the best ways you can use wisdom with men are first, to understand what godly men find appealing (or unappealing). See the section on respect, support, and companionship above for examples. But second, you must think about what you're looking for in a man—and train yourself to look for the right things and back off from the wrong ones. We've all made out that check-list. Some lists are detailed with a host of highly defined specifics; others are merely general outlines. Whatever your list looks like, here are three questions you must check off before making any serious commitment to a man.

1. IS HE A CHRISTIAN?

Scripture clearly forbids Christians from being unequally yoked to non-Christians (2 Cor. 6:14). Those who ignore this directive will eventually regret this spiritual compromise.

In his book *The Clash of Civilizations,* Harvard professor Samuel Huntington predicted in 1996 that the major cause of global conflicts in the future would be religious differences. He based that conclusion on his observation that religion is the heart of every major culture. Religion, he said, is the immovable right-and-wrong viewpoint people passionately cling to and want others to embrace, even if force is sometimes required.

September 11 proved Huntington right. Many of the greatest global tensions in our world occur when the religious belief systems of different cultures are forced to rub against one another. And what's true of cultures is true of people merged by marriage. When people of two different religions marry (even if the "religion" of one is secular or atheistic), trouble will soon arise along the lines where their conflicting religious views meet. It's inevitable. Not because the husband or wife lacks goodwill toward the other but because inevitably one or both will feel pressured, may compromise, may worry, and eventually will begin to resent the other person. As with the sex-before-marriage issue, God's standards are there for a reason; He knows what will come when we are unequally yoked.

2. WHAT WAS HIS HOME LIFE LIKE GROWING UP?

A man's childhood script is probably the script he'll bring with him into your marriage, so the more you know about his upbringing, the better. He'll refer to it unconsciously and automatically when he makes gut reactions or responds to pressure. So as you explore your friendship, ask him about his childhood. Don't make him feel like you're quizzing him (that's a common unintentional signal that you are challenging him, which could feel like disrespect and make a wise man nervous), but do share your past and explore his. Was it good? Difficult? Troubled? What are his most dominant childhood memories? What about his relationships with his parents and siblings? Are they healthy or broken? Who impacted him the most?

Mom? Dad? In what ways? Are there open sores with them that remain unhealed? What was his parents' marriage like? What did he learn from it?

A man's past may be a source of great strength and blessing to your relationship. Good things early in life can go a long way toward ensuring the same later in life. Unfortunately, the opposite is also true. A troubled past may foretell future trouble—especially if he hasn't dealt with it well. The family suitcase a man brings with him may unexpectedly explode in your relationship, leaving you sorting through all kinds of hurt, confusion, strange behaviors, and unfinished business. Or he may keep all the pain there sealed up tight, leaving him mysterious, moody, angry, or demanding.

Unfortunately you can't make him unpack that suitcase. It has to be *his* willingness, *his* commitment; and if he is indeed willing, it speaks well of him. But before marriage you should do a lot of probing. You should discuss how he (and you, for that matter) will handle any difficulties that arise. And if he's not interested in going there, odds are you'll be in for a rocky relationship at some point later on. But don't make that "later on" be "once you are married." Know your man's past and how he will handle it before you commit to marry him, just as you must be willing to make sure he knows yours and how you will handle it before he commits to marry you.

3. WHAT HAS HIS PAST PERFORMANCE BEEN LIKE?

Why this question? Because past performance is your best eye into a man's future performance. So if you're single and dating, look closely at your guy's past performance with you and with other women. Has he been moral or immoral? Has he cared for you, or have you taken care of him? Has he been wild and crazy or steady and predictable? As you've gotten to know him, have you seen a teachable heart when he makes mistakes or hurt your feelings—or a stubborn one? What he has been, he will be again. Can't share his heart and feelings before marriage? Don't kid your-self. That won't change after marriage. Poor work habits before marriage? Same after you're married. Bad finances? Same again. You'll be wresting the checkbook from him and trying to manage the finances before your bank account bottoms out.

We're not saying he *cannot* change. We're only saying not to count on it. A wedding ring will not morph a man into some newly minted white knight. And his wife won't change him either. Only he can change himself. His past—including his demonstrated willingness to make himself into a better man for you—is your best eye into the future.

Wise Moves to Make Now

Let's finish out this chapter by getting ultrapractical about using wisdom with a man in a relationship, day to day. While there are countless things you can do, we believe that the ones listed below are the most important. And for those who are married, these must come in the context of the "biblical marriage" pattern discussed in chapter 4. So take a few minutes to consider how you might need to change your words and actions to uphold your end of a biblical marriage (or prepare for one) in any of these areas.

LOOK FOR THE POSITIVE

Many unhappy marriages are actually pretty good overall. The problem is, husbands and wives tend to get locked in on each other's negatives. They lose sight of all the positive things about their significant other. As someone once told me, "You can blot out the sun with your thumb if you bring it close enough to your eye." You can also blot out a good marriage if you focus only on the things your husband is not. You really don't have to look too hard to find something positive to think about—and *say to*—him.

If you are having trouble respecting your man, we urge you to do the "30 Day Challenge," which Nancy Leigh DeMoss from time to time gives to the listeners of her radio program. She says, essentially, "For the next thirty days, I don't want you to say anything negative about your husband—either *to him* or *about him* to someone else. Nothing negative. And for the next thirty days, I want you to find one thing you can affirm about him and tell him." This is a powerful prescription for helping to lift your eyes from the difficulties and onto those very real factors that are "worthy of praise," as the apostle Paul puts it in Philippians 4:8.

SUPPORT YOUR MAN IN PUBLIC

Proverbs 12:4 says, "An excellent wife is the crown of her husband, but she who shames him is like rottenness in his bones." Nothing can hurt a man more than being criticized by his wife or girlfriend in front of his peers. Even something as "teasing" as rolling your eyes before others to mock his words or behavior can devastate him. The reason? It shouts, "This guy doesn't have it together." He may not react visibly to this sort of thing in the moment, but inside he begins to harbor secret anger and hurt against you for this public shaming. And that anger and hurt will often come out later in a different time and context.

Conversely, though, *nothing* builds a man up more than seeing his wife or girlfriend support him in public. He develops strong feelings of love and gratitude. So show your support for him whenever you can.

CHEER FOR YOUR MAN, EVEN WHEN HE HAS FLAWS

There's no perfect man or perfect marriage. Don't fall into the trap of idealizing other couples and their outwardly perfect marriages. Still, many women embrace marriage perfection in their minds. This mirage unnecessarily undercuts and stokes dissatisfaction in their own marriages.

Many of us struggle to gauge accurately the health of our marriages. Most of us are more pessimistic than we should be, dwelling on the 5 percent that's out of whack to the exclusion of the 95 percent that's on track. But here's the thing: if a man isn't performing well—if his flaws are showing—he *knows* that. He doesn't need anyone to point it out to him. Nagging won't do any good. But he is incredibly motivated to do better when someone believes in him even in the face of mistakes and flaws. A wife's unwavering support will actually help him be the man she's already treating him as!

TAKE SEX SERIOUSLY

For those who are married, remember: it's not about the physical need as much as it is about feeling that you desire him and that he's pleasing you. Stay creative. Surprise him from time to time. Take care of yourself.

Tell him what he's doing right and how good he makes you feel. Good sex is life giving to a husband.

TAKE AN ACTIVE INTEREST IN YOUR MAN'S JOB

As we mentioned before, a man wants to marry a woman who will nourish his life vision. You should have a good hands-on knowledge of all that your boyfriend or husband does and appreciate the pressures he faces. Interact with him when he needs to talk about his work. If he asks (which he will if he sees you as "safe" and not likely to criticize or control), problem-solve with him. Pray for him and let him know it. Be his career partner.

PUT YOUR RELATIONSHIP WITH YOUR HUSBAND BEFORE THAT WITH YOUR KIDS

That is sometimes hard to do as the years go by. You get caught up in all the things the kids are doing, often seeing more of them than you do your husband. What you don't notice is the growing distance developing between you and the man you vowed years ago to give your life to.

Then comes the day when the house is empty of children. They're gone. But so is the closeness between you and your husband. You're alone with a stranger. Don't let that happen. Keep developing new ways to enjoy each other even while the kids are home. Take regular getaways without the children throughout your marriage to renew and refresh your relationship. Keep finding new ways to connect and enjoy life together. And when that day comes when the last kid moves out, you'll be able to turn to your husband and say, "Woohoo! Let the good times roll!"

SEEK HELP FOR ABUSE

Don't be afraid to ask for outside help if there is physical or emotional violence in your marriage or dating relationship. If you're married, remember that marriage is a community project, not a contract of silence. It might be hard to open up to others because you're afraid of what you might lose. But if you have an abusive relationship, what you're holding on to will never get better in secret. Start by opening up to a trusted friend, family member, pastor, or counselor. Let this person give you perspective and then coach you on what to do next. If you are feeling abused, do this now!

Use Your Compass

As we pointed out in the beginning of the chapter, flying by instinct with a man isn't going to be good enough to get us where we want to go. We all need something more to be successful with a man. Proverbs 24:3–4 explains: "By wisdom a house is built, and through understanding it is established; through knowledge its rooms are filled with rare and beautiful treasures" (NIV). You need wisdom to make wise choices, perceptive understanding to give you a firm foundation, and the right knowledge of his real needs to fill your home with delight. This biblical compass, not your instincts, will guide and empower your relationship with your man and thus support every other area of your life.

Before you move on to the next chapter, jot down here any changes you think you need to make to better use wisdom with a man.

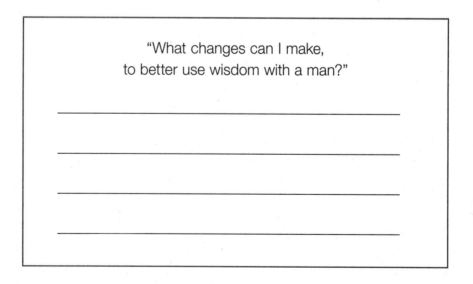

"What changes can I make,
to better use wisdom with a man?"

10

Stewarding Your Gifts from an Eternal Perspective

*I*n the movie *Awakenings*,[1] Dr. Malcolm Sayer discovers that a new drug will awaken people from a decades-long catatonic state. Amid the celebration of this discovery, it soon becomes clear that this "awakening" won't last for long. The same people who are learning to live anew also have to come to terms with the idea that it's only temporary. Imagine that you were in those patients' shoes: the last thing you can remember was when you were twenty, and now you're suddenly fifty years old! You have missed so much, and now you know that you have a limited number of days ahead of you. Would you just sit around, waiting for the inevitable? Or would you make the most of the time you had been given? All of us probably hope that we would have the determination to really *live* during those days or months—to make an impact, to do something meaningful.

This is a great metaphor for our lives as believers in Christ. We only have a limited time here on earth. What a difference it will make if we think of it that way and determine to use that time well. And the best way to make the most of these precious, few years we have been given here is to accomplish the purposes God has laid out for us—not just the big picture callings common to all people but the personal callings He has given each of us as individuals. We will focus in this chapter on these unique, individual, personal callings.

Faith Step #4: Steward Your Gifts from an Eternal Perspective

Our personal callings start with the specific gifts God has given each of us—our individual design specifications, as it were. Think about what some of those gifts are. What do you just love to do—what do you feel alive doing?

Ephesians 2:10 says, "For we are God's workmanship, created in Christ Jesus *to do good works*, which God prepared in advance for us to do" (NIV, emphasis ours). God tells us He has designed us with those unique, individual skills and abilities *for a reason;* they are there to be used for specific purposes and specific works.

God then puts our gifts in context. He says we are also just one part of a bigger picture: the body of Christ. He has designed our individual gifts and callings to fit together with those of everyone else. Our purpose makes up a specific part of the body, without which the rest of the body will not function well. And in the end God intends for the whole body—all His purposes—to be working together to accomplish something great for His glory!

> God tells us He has designed us with those individual abilities for a reason—they are to be used for specific purposes. ∂º

This means that from God's perspective, looking at the big picture, He has some amazing things planned that we can be a part of—that we are *intended* to be a part of! If we are open to what God is doing and follow Him, our personal callings *will* lead us into some exciting and meaningful ministries, great adventures, and special surprises along the way.

We will almost certainly experience some real challenges. God cares even more about who we *are* in Him than about what we *do for* Him. And He knows that the character of His children is usually refined far more in the furnace than in the soft and easy life we would all no doubt prefer! Further, we live in a world that, since Adam and Eve's sin, God has allowed us to be under the temporary authority of the enemy of our souls. And God will waste no lessons that come as a result of that hardship.

The fact is, transforming the darkness of our world with the light of Christ is, in one way or another, the primary point behind the callings and design He has put into us. The difficulties we face in life point us to the urgency of our quest. So actually living out God's callings, accomplishing His purposes, and experiencing the great things He has for us will usually require us to change our perspective and look at our situation from the big picture, and *not* focus on what our circumstances look like in this hour, or this week, or even this year.

As all of us know, that is easier said than done. When you have poured yourself into something and it just doesn't seem to be working, it is easy to get discouraged. But the reason we are discouraged is that we are focusing on what is happening right now. Instead, we need to do what God is asking, trust that He is heading somewhere great, and let the results be up to Him.

I (Shaunti) find this to be just as hard as anyone does, but there have been a few times God has allowed me to see that big picture over time and realize that what looked like a dead end is not that at all and is instead a necessary step in a much grander adventure that we cannot fathom at that moment. Let me give you an example.

About twelve years ago God gave me a miraculous entrée into the publishing world. This was ironic since in my previous career on Wall Street and Capitol Hill, my job evaluations always listed writing as the main area needing improvement. I guess that shows God's transforming power because as I wrote my first books, I did feel God had given me some gifts in the area of writing and speaking. And as children began to come along, writing was also a field in which I could work around my children's schedules and still bring in income to pay off student loans!

Everything was going fine until Jeff and I hit a serious financial bind after the tech crash and 9/11. Jeff had been running a start-up technology company with many employees, but like many other tech-company owners, he had to let his employees go and take no salary while he tried to rebuild the company.

In the middle of that discouraging time, I felt so strongly that God was asking me to write a particular novel on a particular subject. I was convinced that He would make this novel a best seller and—ta-da!—we'd be saved!

I poured myself into writing *The Lights of Tenth Street* for a year, and it hit the shelves . . . and started out by selling very few copies. After a year of work and lots of research costs, it initially *lost* us money. I couldn't understand it. Jeff and I were hitting the pavement looking for work, we didn't know how we were going to pay our mortgage, we had a baby and a toddler, and I was *so* upset. "God," I said, "why did You have me spend that whole year writing that novel? I did so much research, and few people will ever see it! It did *no* good!"

A few months later I was at the Christian publishing industry convention in Orlando, paying my own way to get there, still trying to convince someone—anyone—to do a radio interview, a mention in a newspaper . . . *anything* to promote the book. And there was no interest. It looked like all that work, all that research, all that use of certain abilities that I thought God had *told* me to do, was wasted.

But I was looking at it as if today's circumstance is all that matters. However, God could see the bigger picture. You see, in that novel, one of my main characters was a man. And I had spent a year interviewing men to learn what thoughts to put into my character's head, and I was so surprised by what I was learning.

As I walked down through the convention center on my last day in Orlando, suddenly a title came into my head: *For Women Only: What You Need to Know About the Inner Lives of Men.* And I literally stopped dead in the middle of the hallway, as into my head sprang this entire idea for how to take what I had learned, do even more research, and create a nonfiction book to help women understand men. I thought, "Wow, Lord, that is a really good idea!"

That book came out a year later, and it exploded. It has sold nearly one million copies in eighteen different languages. I'm so in awe that God has used this new understanding to launch, improve, heal, or save hundreds of thousands of marriages! And none of that would have happened if I hadn't written the novel that, at first, lost us money and caused me so much discouragement. It wouldn't have happened if I had focused on what circumstances looked like that year and said, "I quit."

Remember, God has purposes for you, and His purposes lead to many different kinds of results. You don't know what those are going to be—big, small, fun, scary, personal, professional—you discover them along the way. You don't force the impact; God determines it. Remember Ephesians 2:10. God already has a plan for the use of your gifts! Sometimes He will graciously allow us to see the working out of those purposes on this earth; others, we won't know about until we get to heaven. We don't know where our gifts will take us, but we do know that if we don't figure out what our gifts are and use them for Him, we will never experience these things.

The Parable of the Talents

Biblically, using our gifts in the way God has called us to is called good stewardship, and it is stewardship for a specific point and purpose that we often miss. Let's look at a parable about this from Matthew 25.

> [Jesus said:] "For it will be like a man going on a journey, who called his servants and entrusted to them his property. To one he gave five talents, to another two, to another one, to each according to his ability. Then he went away. He who had received the five talents went at once and traded with them, and he made five talents more. So also he who had the two talents made two talents more. But he who had received the one talent went and dug in the ground and hid his master's money. Now after a long time the master of those servants came and settled accounts with them. And he who had received the five talents came forward, bringing five talents more, saying, 'Master, you delivered to me five talents; here I have made five talents more.' His master said to him, 'Well done, good and faithful servant. You have been faithful over a little; I will set you over much. Enter into the joy of your master.' And he also who had the two talents came forward, saying, 'Master, you delivered to me two talents; here I have

made two talents more.' His master said to him, 'Well done, good and faithful servant. You have been faithful over a little; I will set you over much. Enter into the joy of your master.' He also who had received the one talent came forward, saying, 'Master, I knew you to be a hard man, reaping where you did not sow, and gathering where you scattered no seed, so I was afraid, and I went and hid your talent in the ground. Here you have what is yours.' But his master answered him, 'You wicked and slothful servant! You knew that I reap where I have not sown and gather where I scattered no seed? Then you ought to have invested my money with the bankers, and at my coming I should have received what was my own with interest. So take the talent from him and give it to him who has the ten talents. For to everyone who has will more be given, and he will have an abundance. But from the one who has not, even what he has will be taken away. And cast the worthless servant into the outer darkness. In that place there will be weeping and gnashing of teeth.'" (Matt. 25:14–30 ESV)

This parable is a window into something we often don't realize about eternity. The Master gives us, His servants, resources to steward while He is gone. Then He comes back and judges us on how well we used them while He was away. And if we were faithful, He gives us more. But what we often miss is that the "more" is for eternity.

We can learn two overriding principles from the parable of the talents that together give us our Faith Step of stewarding our gifts from an eternal perspective.

We Will Be Held Accountable

First, we will be held accountable for how we steward God's gifts. The most important starting point from this parable is that these talents we have been given *are not ours.* When a master hands a bag of money over to a servant to invest, everyone knows the money doesn't actually belong to the servant. The servant is using it, and he is trying to do something with it, but it is not his. If he does use the money for himself, he's stealing from the master!

In the same way, God gives us our skills and gifts. They ultimately belong to Him, and He asks us to use them for Him and His purposes. If we use them for ourselves instead, or if we claim they are from us instead of from God, we are actually stealing from Him.

Because God has given these gifts for His purposes, when we stand before the Judgment Seat, He will hold us accountable for how well we stewarded what He entrusted to us. And the judgment of "how well" will be from His perspective, not ours! We cannot bury those gifts in the ground and not use them. In the parable, the Master was *angry* with the third servant. All the purposes He'd had for those gifts had been wasted.

Using Our Gifts in the Right Way

All that said, we must use our gifts in the *way* God asks us to use them. This is one important aspect to "how well" we use these gifts (we will cover more in the next section). Just as we must not bury our talents in the ground we must not try to take on *more* than what God has asked of us, or use them in a way God has not designed us for. This is where we come back to all the other points we've covered in this book. Our Core Callings must be the starting point and priority, and everything we do must fit in with and advance them rather than conflict with them.

Jesus Himself provides our ultimate role model in this do-it-all world of not taking on more than what God has asked. He said, "The Son can do nothing by himself; he can do only what he sees his Father doing" (John 5:19 NIV). Think about that. There were people in need whom Jesus Himself did not reach out to because that was not what God was doing at that time! In fact, when the apostle John relays Jesus' statement, he illustrates it by starting with the example of the pool of Bethesda where "a great number of disabled people" congregated to seek healing. And yet that particular Sabbath Jesus *only* spoke to and healed one man! Because, Jesus explained, He could "only do what he sees his Father doing." The lesson that teaches us about similarly listening to the Father and restraining our "do it all" tendencies is *profound*.

If we do more than what God has given to us to do, we will surely end up living a stress-filled life. But when we use our gifts in the ways God has called us, we can say, as Jesus did, "I have brought you glory on earth by completing the work you gave me to do" (John 17:4 NIV).

When You Have Children at Home

As we have done from time to time, let's explicitly address the issue of what "using your gifts" means for you if you are a mom with children at home. In any group of Christian mothers, there are sure to be women who feel strongly that the primary use of their gifts in this season must be as a stay-at-home mom—just as there are sure to be women who feel called to use their gifts beyond the home as well.

If you know you are called to be a stay-at-home mom, and you are doing so, first, thank you for that wonderful step of love and that sacrifice! You are a wonderful role model in a world that *needs* more role models who have responded to that godly calling! Next, though, if you aren't already doing so, take a look at whether God has given you some unused gifts that He might be wanting you to use during this season of life in other "subdue and rule" ways.

For example, I know one stay-at-home mom with preschool-age children who has had the most amazing impact on others' lives because she has used her gift of relationship building and prayer to reach out to other moms in her community, connect on playdates, and then make an offer to pray for the other mom's needs. Today, when those other moms have trouble in a marriage or just want to talk; they call her! Several have come to Christ and are now pouring into their own children from a Christian perspective! What an amazing impact that has come with just one stay-at-home mom' who is looking for ways to use her gift for a "subdue and rule" purpose.

Or perhaps you are in the other situation. Do you have obvious gifts beyond the home, but you feel like you aren't really "allowed" to use them until the kids are grown? You might feel like Lucy, the business owner in my core group who really struggled with the idea of the Core Callings at first. She said, "When I look at other women that have given up their careers and their gifts and their talents to bring up their children, I wonder if they are selling themselves short. What do you say when you go and stand before God and say, 'Yeah, I had all these gifts and talents, and I did nothing with them'? I think that it's not possible that God could have created us and put all these things in us and then said, 'No, don't do that.' . . . I think if I have this gift, I'm going to maximize and make the most of it because I don't want to sit there at the end of my life and think, *Why did I waste it?* I don't want it all to be for naught."

As we've noted before, many of the latter group feel pressured or guilty, as if they are not *allowed* to use their gifts outside the home until the kids are older. But a more biblical view is the recognition that there is no one-size-fits-all answer to *how* each person fulfills the Core Callings. God has given specific gifts to each specific individual, to be used for specific purposes—but *the way in which* we use those gifts will often differ depending on our season of life and other factors. We have to do as Jesus did and listen for what the Father is doing. And we can take this to the bank: God would never give us a purpose that would prevent our being able to fulfill our "be fruitful and multiply" calling with our own children.

This is because the most important gift any of us will ever receive from God to steward is children. Think about this for a second: this human life has been lovingly fashioned by the Master—and then the Master takes this new life and instead of jealously guarding it and protecting it *from* lunkheads like us, He hands this life *to* us for the most formative years of existence!

My first publisher told me the story of when he let his little five-year-old son go on his first overnight trip to his uncle's house. He was so nervous about leaving his little boy, and as he drove away, he prayed, "Lord, I just have to trust You with my son." He instantly felt like God replied, "You have to trust him with *Me?! You* have to trust him with *Me?!* I have to trust him with *you*, buddy!"

That puts it in perspective! Ultimately, these "talents" that we've been given—children, skills, money, and so on—belong to God, not us. He *is* truly trusting us with them. And He will hold us accountable for stewarding all of them well.

If We Are Faithful, We Will Be Given More

The second principle we can draw from the parable of the talents is that if we are faithful with what we've been given in this life, more will be given to us in eternity. This parable is often misunderstood as saying that if you're faithful in small things this year, you'll be given bigger or more things next year. Now, just to be clear, rewarding faithfulness is absolutely in God's character; and indeed, many times, if more opportunities keep coming your way, it is *because* you have been faithful with the starting point, and God knows He can trust you with more. But although that is true, that is not what this specific parable is about.

For the servants in the parable, the "more" is given *after* the master comes back. Think about that for a moment. Jesus is saying the reckoning and the giving of more gifts will happen *after He returns*!

So He comes back, the world is at an end, He looks at how you as a Christian have used the gifts He gave you, and if you've been faithful with them, He gives you many times more.

So when do you use all these new gifts He has given you? The only possible answer is that you use them in eternity. What this means is that your experience of eternity is going to be shaped by your stewardship of what you've been given in this life! To be clear: this is not about *whether* you will spend eternity in heaven because God says that has to do with knowing and loving Him and has nothing to do with how much you do for Him. (In the parable the third servant who was cast into the darkness clearly did not know his master and his character at all.) Instead, this is talking about *what* your experience in heaven will be like.

This is a radical concept for most of us to grasp because, to be frank, we in the Christian community spend little time focusing on the concept of living in heaven. It is almost as if entering heaven is the end point, and our ultimate goal is getting to it. But if we think about it, we know that is completely wrong! We know getting to heaven isn't the end point! Heaven is just the beginning of an amazing new season of life that will last forever.

Think about the sheer number of times Jesus tried to move our focus from getting *to* heaven and instead include living *in* heaven. For example: "Do not store up for yourselves treasures on earth, where moth and rust destroy, and where thieves break in and steal. But store up for yourselves treasures in heaven" (Matt. 6:19–20 NIV). Or, "In my Father's house are many rooms. . . . I am going there to prepare a place for you" (John 14:2–3 NIV).

It's the same type of mistake many brides make if they spend all their time focusing on preparing for the wedding, which will be here and done in a flash, instead of for the marriage, which will last for the rest of their life. Well, guess what? We are preparing for the ultimate marriage of Jesus and His bride—us!—in eternity! It is so easy to focus solely on this short life on earth instead of recognizing that the Bible says that *what* we do in this short life will shape *how* we experience the unimaginable span of eternity.

If we can't grasp that concept or feel uncomfortable with it, our vision of heaven is probably too vague. We think of heaven as this dreamy perfect place, but that is about as far as our vision goes. But we won't be floating around on clouds; we'll be *living*. We'll be working, and praying, and worshipping, and spending amazing amounts of time continuing old relationships and building new ones! And what we do here, *before* the wedding, so to speak, will shape what life looks like after the wedding.

If you can't imagine how heaven would look different for some people than for others, here's a mythical analogy:

Life path one. Suppose you had a unique ability and passion for music as a kid, but during the few years you were a child, you didn't have the desire to do much with it beyond some lessons, singing in the choir and playing in a band in school. You enjoyed it but didn't really want to spend so much time on lessons. A few short years later, you went off to college and then an interesting office job. Today, decades later, you still really love music, and you help lead worship at church. You also accept a few opportunities to sing at weddings and such. But most of your life is focused on enjoying your family and your job.

Now imagine *life path two.* Suppose you had a particular ability and passion for music as a kid, . . . and from the time you were a small child you were, for some reason, unusually focused and diligent about every lesson and every possible opportunity to sing and play. You enjoyed having fun, like any other kid, but nothing could keep you from your two hours of practice each day. You started sending off demo recordings to Christian music companies at age twelve, and at age sixteen signed your first contract. You worked incredibly hard and carefully on that first album, agreed to be homeschooled on the road so you could accept every little invitation to promote your music, and got so much buzz going that the album was a runaway hit. So you put out another one at age eighteen, which is when a major Christian concert promoter called and put you on a thirty-city tour. You took a break for college (spending summers on tour), met your husband along the way, and today your whole family spends six months out of the year touring with you, as you play to concert arenas of ten thousand or more people a night. You are impacting millions each year with your music, visiting the most exotic locations around the world with a loving family, and living a life that most people couldn't imagine.

So here's the question: based on the choices you made in this scenario during the few years when you were a child, how different is your life after that point? Quite a bit different! You enjoy all the years after that in either case. But in the second scenario, your purposeful work to steward your talents as a child led not only to a great reward in terms of impact, but quite frankly to just a totally different experience of life from that point on.

In a way, that is how different heaven will be for us depending on how we steward our gifts here on earth. Jesus essentially said, "To those who use well what they are given before I return, even more will be given after I return, and they will have an abundance" (v. 29).

Now, unlike the earthly notion of a glamorous life of playing to ten-thousand-seat stadiums, we have no idea what "an abundance" will look like in heaven! All we know is that it will be very cool.

Questions about Gifts

So are you motivated to figure out how to be a good steward of the gifts and talents God has given you? You're likely asking several key questions.

How Do We Discern What Our Gifts Are?

Many systems and services are available to help you chart your personal and professional gifts, but as a shortcut, the easiest way to know your gifts is to identify those things that you simply enjoy doing, are passionate about and good at, and tend to do naturally. Your God-given gifts will probably be things you would want to spend *more* time doing if money was no object and that people tend to compliment you on.

For example, when I was testing my eight-session *Life Ready* study with a group of about twenty women, we had not planned on refreshments other than coffee. But one woman, whom I will call Annabelle, showed up for the second session with a pan of homemade shortbread brownies in her hands. And they went really quick! For the third session she brought homemade berry cobbler, and so on. No one asked her to; she just did it! Everyone loved eating the goodies, and Annabelle really enjoyed making and bringing them. You know what? That is an outworking of an innate gift of hospitality.

When you think about the gifts you have that you can use for eternity, don't limit yourself to just the spiritual gifts you find listed in the Bible. Those are obviously great gifts to use, but you can use practically any talent in ways that will glorify God and be a testimony for Him. Take Eric Liddell, for example. Many of you have heard of this man from the Academy Award-winning movie *Chariots of Fire*. Liddell refused to run in the 1924 Olympics on a Sunday due to his Christian beliefs. He later became a missionary to China, but he is most remembered for his running and his Christian witness during the Olympics. Liddell understood that using his gifts for God wasn't just limited to traditional ministry. His sister was pressuring him to stop racing and step into his evangelistic calling to China. He said, "I believe God made me for a purpose—for China. But

He also made me fast! And when I run, I feel His pleasure. To give that up would be to hold Him in contempt. . . . To win is to honor Him."[2]

Who knows how God might use your gifts? But if He gave them to you, it is *so that* you can use them for Him. Thus, if there is a gift that you know God has given to you, and you aren't sure of how to use it for kingdom impact, pray about it and see where God leads you. Paul said that our ultimate ambition, whether here or in heaven, should be to please God.

> Who knows how God might use your gifts? But if He gave them to you, it is *so that* you can use them for Him.

"Therefore we also have as our ambition . . . to be pleasing to Him" (2 Cor. 5:9). Similarly, be open to where you feel like the use of your gifts is pleasing to Him. If you feel like He's calling you to a particular use of a gift, step out, even if you can't figure out how He's going to use it for the kingdom. What gift, when you use it, causes you to "feel His pleasure"? Ask God if that's something He wants you to use now. If you feel that it is, trust that He has a plan and, like Eric Liddell, join the adventure of watching what will happen when you do.

Where Are We to Steward Our Gifts?

The short answer of where to steward our gifts is: anywhere God directs us *that will invest in eternal purposes rather than earthly ones.* Ephesians says God has given us these gifts to (1) go out into the world and minister to others in the name of Christ and to (2) help build up the body of Christ within the church as well. God needs our gifts to do both. The longer answer is that understanding where to use these gifts for the best kingdom purposes will likely require a time of exploration and testing at first.

You might think, "I could never use *my* gift to advance God's kingdom." Yes, you can; it is a matter of being purposeful about kingdom purposes. Annabelle's church, for example, needs more ways to draw newcomers into the church community. Imagine the impact if Annabelle were to use her natural gift of hospitality to invite church visitors over for lunch after church on Sundays!

Now some of us might think, *Oh no, . . . that sounds like a lot of work.* Well, that's actually the point: for someone like Annabelle, because this is her gift, it *doesn't* feel like a lot of work. Someone with the gift of hospitality loves doing that sort of thing and just may never have thought about the many ways she can do what she loves *and* make a purposeful kingdom impact.

To figure out where to use our gifts, we need to look for stewardship "sweet spots." That is where we are advancing God's kingdom . . . and we like what we're doing! These are activities in which, by using our gifts, we come alive. These are areas for which we feel our gifts were designed. Frederick Buechner hit the nail on the head when he said, with amazing insight, "The place God calls you to is the place where your deep gladness and the world's deep hunger meet."[3]

Take a few minutes to make a list of a few gifts you believe God has entrusted to you—those things you just naturally enjoy and are good at. Then try to identify where you might best use these gifts for an eternal investment. These are your stewardship sweet spots. Describe a few of them even if you are not actively using your gifts in this way at the moment. Finally, write down how you feel about where you are in stewarding each of those gifts and whether there's something more you should consider.

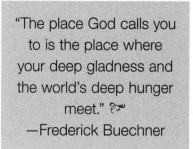

"The place God calls you to is the place where your deep gladness and the world's deep hunger meet."
—Frederick Buechner

Why Are We to Steward Our Gifts?

So why are we to steward our gifts in the first place? This leads us to the second part of our Faith Step—not just stewarding our gifts but doing so from an eternal perspective. The job of a steward is to advance the purposes of the master—to be successful from the *master's* perspective, not necessarily from a servant's perspective.

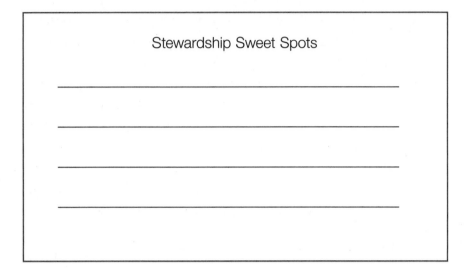

So what is our Master's perspective? It is an eternal perspective about eternal value.

Take a look at the Master's words at the end of the parable, where Jesus talks about throwing the worthless servant outside, into the darkness. It's helpful to understand that this parable is part of a sermon about the last days and how we won't know the day or the hour of Christ's return. Immediately after this parable of the talents, Jesus talks about the sheep and the goats—about His judgment seat.

In context, the parable of the talents is entirely about being a good steward of the life God has given us because one day we will all stand before God and give an account for it. Not *in order to* be saved, but *regardless* of whether or not we are saved. And when each of us comes before Christ on that day, an awful lot of what we're working hard for, spending our time on, and using our gifts for will likely look unimportant because it really did not have all that much value in the Master's eyes. On that day everything everyone has done will be tested, and all that will matter—all that will remain—is what God values in light of eternity. The rest will burn away (2 Cor. 5:10; 1 Cor. 3:12–15).

Understand that it's not bad to focus on some of the daily things of life, on activities and careers and plans and reading magazines and watching a movie with the family. They aren't bad things in themselves. They're not sinful; they aren't wicked. But some aspects of these things are solely of earthly value. For example, I (Shaunti) have a guilty pleasure: reading thriller novels I've read many times before. Reading those is relaxing, and I don't think it is at all "sinful." I don't think God begrudges me that mindless time. Yet the fact remains that the time I spend that way will presumably be one of those things that burns away.

On the other hand, some of the simple things that we don't prioritize are of *great* eternal value. When I go out with Jeff and some friends for dinner, I truly enjoy hearing about their lives and having fellowship and building them up. You know what? That won't burn away: that has eternal value! That is Christian fellowship and ministering to and loving others. There's no reason going and sitting with friends in a movie instead would be bad, but sometimes being able to spend those two hours just talking and supporting each other is even better.

This eternal perspective really helps when you are faced with different choices of how to spend your time. It completely changes our thinking when we ask ourselves: Is there eternal value in this?

A final reason we need to steward our gifts well is one we already mentioned: in heaven, God will reward those who have been faithful in stewarding their gifts while on earth. We are literally building up treasures in heaven. Now many of us have heard that phrase a hundred times, and we think, *Yeah, yeah, treasures in heaven.* But really stop and look at that phrase.

It doesn't mean eternal life; it's an actual reward of some kind once in eternity. It can't mean money since money will have no value in heaven. Instead, we will be experiencing something we will really value once we get there, even if we cannot fathom what that looks like right now.

> This eternal perspective really helps when you are faced with different choices of how to spend your time. It completely changes our thinking when we ask ourselves: Is there eternal value in this?

A New Perspective of Who We Are on Earth

A former pastor of mine (Shaunti's) used to say, "Our main problem as believers is that we often don't really understand the reality of heaven and of eternity. We don't know who we really are. If we did, it would change everything. Everything unimportant would go away, and we would have an automatic, laser focus on living for God in the short time we have here and focusing our gifts only on those things that God says really matter."

The first perspective we need is that we do not belong to this world. The book of Hebrews says we are "aliens and strangers" in this world (11:13 NIV). In other words, we are actually citizens of heaven. I hope you either have a strong view of heaven or have been developing one during this chapter. But if you don't, you should. Eternity is a big deal. It should make an impact on how you live every day.

The second perspective we need is much more sobering, but it is very real. The Bible says that until Christ returns "the whole world lies in the power of the evil one" (1 John 5:19). Essentially, we are living in occupied territory—territory that is ruled by an evil power that wants to kill and steal and destroy. But what we need to realize is that we aren't just "living in" that occupied territory. Once we commit our lives to Christ, we change sides, so to speak. We move from dark to light. So from that moment on, we become God's soldiers for a different kingdom. And by living out God's calling in our lives, with the gifts He has given us, we are *actively working to undermine* the dark authority that rules the world we are living in. So from that moment on, we essentially have a target on our heads.

My pastor used to compare Christians to underground espionage agents. We are like the French underground in World War II, and it helps to look at ourselves and our earthly lives from that perspective. For example, why are we surprised when trouble comes? Would it *ever* have surprised a member of the WWII underground if someone shot at them? No. Because they *knew* that the evil dictator would be trying to take them out.

Furthermore, every hour of every day they knew what had value and what didn't, for suddenly only a few ultimate goals mattered: working to advance the rightful kingdom and fight the plans of the wrongful one—including rescuing those the evil ones had scheduled for destruction.

Do you think the members of the French resistance spent a lot of time worrying about how much they were advancing in their careers or about matching the neighbors' lifestyle? Or worrying about church politics? Or planning their next vacation? Or spending a lot of time obsessing about the latest argument with their spouse? Most of those things aren't innately bad or wrong to think about, but it would have seemed dangerously irrelevant to spend a lot of time or energy on them when, for example, they knew they had only a short window in which to try to rescue the Jews in their neighborhood before they were sent to the prison camps.

Ironically, a few years after I heard that analogy from my pastor, he went on to become an underground worker in a hostile country. He and his wife and children had a huge impact . . . and huge challenges. They woke up one night with men in their bedroom wearing hoods and carrying hatchets. They were savagely attacked, and although my pastor was able to fight them off, his wife nearly lost her life. She was beaten so badly she spent a year in another country learning to talk and walk again. And then when she had recovered, the family moved right back to where they had been living before.

They actually experienced what many of us live every day but never realize: by investing our gifts for God, we are fighting against the power of this world on behalf of another kingdom. And since we have a target on our heads regardless, we might as well be purposeful about it.

> If God has put you somewhere, you do not need to leave that place to go "into ministry" and do what matters. You can do what matters for eternity right where you are. ࿔

We need to purposefully ask, "Am I working to advance God's kingdom on this earth with my gifts?" That will help us avoid the seductive call of what the world says to focus on. In the end those purposeful decisions are the ones that the rightful King will most applaud when He comes back and looks at what we've done and says those words we all long to hear: "Well done, my good and faithful servant."

If God has put you somewhere, you do not need to leave that place to go "into ministry" and do what matters. You can do what matters for eternity right where you are, because it's not about the numbers but about your faithfulness. If you are an inner-city mom who raises or mentors one child at a time well in a challenging environment as God asks you to, you will be rewarded and honored in heaven just as any pastor or missionary will be. It's not about the amount of effect that you can see, but the amount of faithfulness. In the parable of the talents, the first two stewards were given different amounts of talents, but since they both were faithful, they both received double the reward.

So before we go any further . . . how are you doing at stewarding your gifts from an eternal perspective? If there are any changes you feel you are supposed to make, jot those down here.

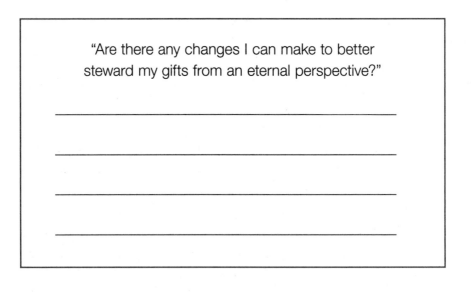

"Are there any changes I can make to better steward my gifts from an eternal perspective?"

_____

_____

_____

_____

Would You Feel Confident Meeting God Today?

Evaluating how we are doing brings us right back to the parable of the talents. But now let's put ourselves in that parable. Let's say that we are the servants. The Master has given each of us these talents and has gone away, but we know He will return. So let us ask an important question.

If the Master were to come back today, would you feel confident in meeting Him? Are you eagerly looking forward to the Master's arrival because you know down deep that you have done the best job you can with what He handed you? You haven't always done it perfectly—no one will—but you have been as faithful as you know how. As you have read this chapter, you may be encouraged because you realize you would be confident in meeting Him! You haven't gotten acclaim in the eyes of the world, but you *have* been a "good and faithful steward" of the priorities that matter most to the Master.

However, some of you wouldn't feel comfortable, and the question is, Why not? One reason may be because of the way you are using, or not using, the gifts the Master has given you. You may be thinking, *I don't know that I have been using my gifts the right way. I've only been using my gifts to bless me!* Or, *I've only been using my gifts on things that have no value in the eyes of the Master.* Or maybe you're realizing you haven't really been using your gifts at all. If any of these are your thoughts, then it is so good you're realizing this now. This would be a great time to talk to someone about how you're living your Christian life, or get into a follow-up Bible study on learning more about spiritual gifts, or ask someone at church for areas you might volunteer.

But there is a second possibility of why you might not feel quite as confident in meeting the Master: is it because you are unsure in your relationship with Him? Maybe you've been thinking, *I'm using my gifts, but I'm not sure of where I am in my relationship with God.* If that's the case with you, then let's stop right here and talk about that. It is so important to realize that our relationship with God is not about what we do, but about what He has already done. It does not depend on using our gifts well but on accepting God's most important gift—the gift of new life.

It is so easy to slip into the idea of using our gifts to "be a good person" and hope the good will outweigh the bad, essentially to try to be good enough for God. But God says that focus will always lead us astray because it is an entirely worldly perspective and is not what He is looking for from us. The truth is, we can *never* be "good enough." Every one of us has some selfishness and sin in our hearts. It is as if every one of us has been kidnapped by sin, and on our own we can never be free of the penalty of death.

But look anew at the most famous verse in the Bible: John 3:16. "For God so loved the world that he gave his only Son, so that everyone who believes in him will not perish but have eternal life" (NLT). Yes, we have been kidnapped by sin, but Jesus (God the Son) loved us so deeply that He laid down His life to pay the ransom *for* us and set us free. A relationship with God starts with simply believing in Jesus, accepting what He has done out of His great love for you, and giving your life over to Him in return.

If this is a new concept to you, if you've never officially given your life to Christ, or if you're simply unsure, now is the time for you to be sure. You don't have to understand everything about how it all works in order to take the essential step of giving your life to God. You can do that by praying—and honestly meaning—the following prayer. Please, if you have never done this before, pray it now:

"Jesus, thank You for Your love for me. I want to get to heaven. I want to live with You forever. I know in so many ways that I live for myself and not for You. Please forgive me. Please wash me free of my sin, free of my selfishness. Thank You for what You have done for me. I accept that, and I will follow You. I give You my life. Please, make me a new person. I want to live for You for the rest of my life here on earth and then live forever with You in heaven."

If you have prayed that prayer, welcome to the family of Christ! Romans 10:13 says, "*Everyone* who calls on the name of the Lord will be saved" (NIV). Or if this wasn't clear to you, please reach out to a Christian friend or church leader to find out more. Then learn how to live, for the rest of your life, in a way that will store up treasures for you in heaven.

11

Believing God, Not Your Fear

*W*e have been presenting a vision for finding God's best for our lives by heading toward the place where our design and our callings as people, as women, and as individuals all line up. So far, we have talked about four of the five Faith Steps we will need to take to get there.

We found that we must prioritize God's callings on our lives and live from the inside out. We were reminded that Ecclesiastes says there are different seasons for everything, and we must be willing to embrace a big-picture understanding of life and live wisely according to the season of life we are in. Because our relationships with men often affect everything else in our lives, including how or whether we fulfill God's purposes, we must also use wisdom with them, understanding and relating to men the way the Bible directs. And in the previous chapter we saw that God has given each of us gifts to use to advance His kingdom, and we must choose to steward our gifts from an eternal perspective rather than just an earthly one.

The fifth Faith Step builds on each of these and is where the rubber meets the road for most of us. Whereas the first four steps tell us what to do, our fifth Faith Step tells us *how* to do those things.

Faith Step #5: Believe God, Not Your Fear

By this point, I (Shaunti) would almost guarantee that almost every one of us has things we feel like we're *supposed* to do, based on what we've learned. So why don't we just do those things? If there's a step you haven't taken—or don't want to take!—I'll bet your reason is a lot like mine.

I'll be transparent: as I was examining the Core Callings and developing this study and book, I felt so convicted that although I was doing okay on "subdue and rule," I needed to do something specific to help me better fulfill my "leave and cleave" and "be fruitful and multiply" callings. I knew God was asking me to finish work and be fully available to my family each day from the point when I picked the kids up from school at 3:00. Literally, no checking my computer for "just one more e-mail," no making "just one more phone call," and certainly no giving in to the temptation to spend an extra hour or two working after the kids were in bed instead of being with my husband. God's directive to me was very clear. So why didn't I just do that?

Well, . . . I just had too much work to do! I had deadlines, and my weekly column had to get done, and I was so behind on my next book, and I had people waiting for what *I* was supposed to deliver so they could do what *they* need to do. . . .

So ultimately, the reason I wasn't following the other Faith Steps was fear. I was afraid that if I did what God had asked me to do, I wouldn't be able to get everything done.

The fact is that we all, at one time or another, simply don't trust God. We're all tempted to think, *If I obey God, I don't believe that He'll work it all out for my best.* The truth is that if we truly trusted Him, we would be able to let go of our fears, do what we know He wants us to do, and believe He will work it all out—regardless of what it looks like.

The Bottom Line: Trust

Most of our objections to doing what we know we are supposed to do come down to this one thing: trusting God. Suppose you are older, and your kids are grown, and you always felt like you were supposed to pursue this one dream that God put in your heart, but you don't know how you would support yourself if you did. . . . That is a trust issue.

If you feel God asking you to step aside from your high-powered role at work into a supporting role while you have children but are worried about whether the high-powered track will still be there for you in five years, . . . that's a trust issue.

If you are single and feel convicted that you need to look for opportunities to build Christian fellowship with more single men but are holding back because there just don't seem to be many good Christian men out there, . . . that's a trust issue.

The great thing is that if we make a decision to trust, God will show us how trustworthy He is.

I have a friend whom I will call Mary, who has had to make a difficult trust choice. Before I met her, Mary was married to a man who was a bit older and whose children were grown, and she never had children of her own. So she poured herself into being salt and light in corporate America and in enjoying her husband. But a few years later that got really difficult. He had some major gifting in business but started to have emotional breakdowns and was diagnosed with depression and other major emotional and mental illnesses. He had to leave his job, and Mary became the sole financial supporter of the family. And because her husband felt like a failure as a man—like he was failing *her*—things got even worse. He was often unstable and angry. Even though he was trying as best he could, medications and counseling were not having much effect, and life became difficult for both of them.

Mary was working all the time and crying all the time; she felt isolated, exhausted, and lonely. After years of this, many of her friends said, "You know, this is an extraordinary situation; and there are times when you just have to leave." But Mary knew God asks us not to leave just because things get difficult. She knew she had vowed "for better or for worse," and even though she loved him, at the moment it definitely felt like "for worse." There was no physical abuse (that changes everything), but it was just very hard.

Every time Mary prayed, she felt God quietly affirm that His job for her was to be this man's wife, that her husband needed her, that he couldn't help being sick any more than he could help it if he had contracted diabetes or cancer, and that she needed to decide to make a firm commitment no matter what. She also felt God was telling her that she couldn't do it alone; she needed to put structures in place to support that decision for the long haul. She especially needed Christian fellowship, support, and friendships, whether or not her husband participated.

She was so afraid. "God," she asked, "will it be like this for the rest of my life?" She felt like God was giving her no guarantees; all she had was the directive of where to start. So Mary decided to believe God, not her fear. She reached out to people at church to establish friendships and get support. She joined our home group, and then her husband started coming, too.

As the years went by, it was still difficult, but Mary wasn't alone. She was trying. And her husband was trying as best he could, too. After many years God brought him both a new type of psychiatrist and a volunteer position that he is passionate about, which helps give him a sense of purpose and ease his depression a bit. Things are still hard. God has not healed Mary's husband, and living with emotional and mental illness is really tough for both of them. But things are much better than they were just a few years ago. Mary has seen the fruit that comes from stepping out in faith and believing that God would help her "leave and cleave" well.

The Choice Has Consequences

Some pretty significant consequences flow out of the choice of whether to believe God and His Word or whether to believe our fear.

Look at the children of Israel. They had a real problem trusting God. God had told them He would bring them out of Egypt to a land flowing with milk and honey. But whenever things got bad, when Pharaoh made things harder on them, when they saw the Red Sea and no way across, when they saw the desert with no food or water, when they saw the giants in the new land, what did they do? Their belief in God utterly failed, and they did not obey Him, . . . and there was a progression to their lack of faith.

The passage in 2 Kings 17:6–18 opens with the history that the Israelites were overthrown and deported to Assyria and that this happened "because the Israelites had sinned against the LORD their God." So what did they do? Take a look at this list.

> They worshiped other gods and followed the practices of the nations the LORD had driven out before them. . . . The Israelites secretly did things against the LORD their God that were not right. From watchtower to fortified city they built themselves high places in all their towns. They set up sacred stones and Asherah poles on every high hill and under every spreading tree. At every high place they burned incense, as the nations whom the LORD had driven out before them had done. . . . They forsook all the commands of the LORD their God. . . . They bowed down to all the starry hosts, and they worshiped Baal. They sacrificed their sons and daughters in the fire. They practiced divination and sorcery and sold themselves to do evil in the eyes of the LORD, provoking him to anger. So the LORD was very angry with Israel and removed them from his presence. (NIV)

Why this amazing slide? How did they go from worshipping God to adopting a few customs from nearby cultures to practicing sorcery and sacrificing their babies to demons?! Verse 14: They, like their fathers, "*did not trust in the LORD their God.*"

Here's how it worked for them—which is how it can all too easily work for all humanity. God said to do something, but the Israelite people did not trust Him, so they didn't obey Him. Since they didn't actually step out to do what He'd asked them to do, they didn't see His hand at work and thus didn't have their faith strengthened; instead, they weakened their trust even more. So when they got to the Promised Land, they eventually stopped following God's commandments and started sliding away from Him. The further from Him they drifted, the easier it was to slide into that easy path of absorbing the customs of the nations around them—which eventually included the worship of false, evil gods. In the end they were so far down that road that they actually killed their own children.

It didn't go from believing and trusting God one day to worshipping demons and killing their children the next. Instead it started with not really believing God, and it went downhill from there.

It is so easy for that same type of downward slide to be at work in our lives if we aren't careful.

Suppose you feel like God wants you to take a hard step, but you can't see how it will work out. You're afraid. Instead of exercising faith, you don't do what God asks you to do. So you don't see Him come through, which would strengthen your faith next time. Instead, you take matters into your own hands and try to make something else work, and you start depending on yourself, which makes you trust God even less. Because you trust God less, you drift from Him. Then, it becomes all too easy to start ignoring His small commandments and begin living your life without God. Inevitably, the further you get from Him and the less you rely on Him, the more likely you are to slide into ignoring big commandments. Once you ignore things you are supposed to do, it is also all too easy to start actively doing things you *aren't* supposed to do. You find yourself breaking His commandments and embracing ways that are ungodly.

Without originally intending to, you have ended up on a path to serious regrets. And it all started with listening to fear instead of practicing faith.

We are all either moving up toward a closer and richer walk with God, or we're making decisions that move us away. Isaiah 7:9 puts it this way: "If you do not stand firm in your faith, you will not stand at all" (NIV).

Role Models for Believing God

Thankfully, in the Bible we don't just see examples of those who didn't exercise faith. We also find so many encouraging examples of people who are great role models for trusting and believing God and the blessing that comes from that choice! When you get a chance, look at the amazing list of names in Hebrews 11. Every one of those men and women have a story of faith and obeying God even when it was difficult.

Let's take a look at one of them—Abraham. Hebrews 11:8–9 says, "It was by faith that Abraham obeyed when God called him to leave home and go to another land that God would give him as his inheritance. He went without knowing where he was going. And even when he reached the land God promised him, he lived there by faith—for he was like a foreigner, living in tents" (NLT). Have you ever thought, *If I obey God, how will I support myself? How will I pay my bills?* It's likely Abraham did also. But he went anyway. In the story of Abraham, Genesis 15:6 says, "Abram *believed* the LORD, and the LORD counted him as righteous because of his faith" (NLT, emphasis added).

It would have been easy for Abraham to say, "Absolutely, I'll go, once I can see where I'm going and how I will support myself once I get there. I'll go once I save up some money to live off of." In other words: "I'll go once I can trust myself. I'll go once I don't *have* to trust God."

> Each of us has to fight the tendency to trust ourselves and not trust God, especially since the areas that are hardest to trust God in are the most important for us! ❧

Each of us has to fight that natural, sinful tendency to trust ourselves and not trust God, especially since some of the areas that will be the hardest to trust God in are the most important for us!

Where Do You Need to Trust?

So the question is: In which areas or situations do you need to trust God? Is it something about your work? Your children? Your marriage? Your ministry? Take a few minutes to think about the directives you feel God has given you, in which you need to trust Him—especially as they relate to the Core Callings and Faith Steps. This is something participants will be doing in detail in the *Life Ready Woman Study*, but you can make a start here using the charts you've filled out at the end of chapters 6, 8, 9, and 10. There may be actions you know you should commit to, but you're fearful or worried and are having a hard time letting go and trusting God with them—like, for example, my fear that if I truly stopped all work at

3:00 p.m. to spend time with my kids and husband, that I wouldn't meet my deadlines. Put those into words in the box below.

In each area where you know you need to trust God, put into words the fear that is holding you back. What are you afraid will happen if you do what you know you are supposed to do? This is probably going to be a difficult statement like, "I'm afraid that if I do this, I'll lose my job," or, "I'm scared that this will make me feel powerless."

Then consider the trusting alternative that is actually true even if you don't feel it. For example, if you're worried about your finances, it would be, "God can take care of my family financially. I can trust Him to be faithful."

Finally, think about what you could do (or are already doing) to move from a lack of trust to actually believing God and obeying Him. This will be a precise action step or series of actions that will lead you toward obedience. For example, "I will pray each day for the next four weeks about whether I really am supposed to cut back on my work hours. If I continue to feel that way, I *will* take steps to cut back hours, cut back expenses, and see how God makes a way."

- "What step is God asking me to take, in which I need to trust Him?"

- "What am I afraid will happen if I do this?"

- "By contrast, what is God's truth (even if I don't feel it)?"

- "What action step(s) should I take now?"

It really is encouraging once you go through this exercise, take the steps you are supposed to take despite your fear, and watch what God does. For me, I literally could not fathom how I would get everything done if I completely stopped work at 3:00 p.m., but since I felt this was what God was asking of me, I simply had to obey and trust that He would work it out somehow. And I have seen that *each time* I made that hard choice, God either gave me amazing efficiency to get the work done in the time I had *or* worked it out another way. You would not believe the number of times I have, for example, nervously approached a strict-deadlines editor for a magazine to say something like, "I know I was supposed to get this article to you by Wednesday, but I'm running a bit behind. Can I possibly have a few more days?" And they would say, "Well, it turns out that I am slammed on another project and can't review it until Friday afternoon anyway, so that is fine." Amazing.

I will never be perfect in this area. There are still times I give into fear and have to go back and apologize to God (and my kids!). But my faith has been strengthened by seeing how God works it out when we do what He asks.

Three Steps to Believing God

Now that we've identified some specific things we need to trust God with, *how* do we do that? How do we move past our fear and to faith? When we look to our compass of God's Word, we find a prescription for overcoming fear and building trust and belief in Him. There are three key steps to this prescription.

Cultivate Your Relationship with God

First, we have to be in an ongoing, sincere relationship with God through His Word. Do you think it is easier or harder to hear from God and trust Him when He asks you to do something, when you are close to Him or when you are far from Him? The answer is obvious. It's out of our relationship with God that we will know who He really is and be able to hear Him direct us.

Let's talk about "knowing who He really is" for a moment. Look at Isaiah 26:3–4: "You will keep in perfect peace all who trust in you, all whose thoughts are fixed on you! Trust in the LORD always, for the LORD GOD is the eternal Rock" (NLT). If you truly know who He is—that He is the Rock eternal, the majestic, all-powerful Creator of the heaven and the earth, you'll have a lot easier time trusting. And if we trust, Isaiah says, "He will keep us in perfect peace."

Part of knowing who God is also involves knowing that His ways are higher than ours and His plans for our life may be different from what we would have chosen. As Isaiah 55:8 says, "'For My thoughts are not your thoughts, nor are your ways My ways,' declares the LORD." We have to submit to that. There's a great line in the movie *Rudy* where the main character is confused about why he's not getting his dream when he has prayed so hard. The priest answers, "Son, in thirty-five years of religious study, I have only come up with two hard incontrovertible facts: there is a God, and I'm not Him."[1]

The other reason it is important to be in relationship with God is that we will be better able to hear from Him. Look at how Jesus put it in John 10. "The man who enters by the gate is the shepherd of his sheep. . . . His sheep follow him because they know his voice. But they will never follow a stranger; in fact, they will run away from him because they do not recognize a stranger's voice. . . . I am the good shepherd; I know my sheep and my sheep know me" (John 10:2–5, 14 NIV).

We have been learning that there are a lot of different directions we can go with our lives, according to all our different callings. But we can't just make decisions on our own and think God will bless them. We have to be close to Him, pray, listen, and read His Word every day so that we can hear what *He* is doing in our lives and join Him in it.

Act on Trust, Not Feelings

The second part of the biblical prescription for trust is: Once we hear from God, we have to make a *decision* to believe and trust, regardless of how we feel or whether we understand why. God understands how hard it is to trust when we don't feel like it. Remember, He has lived it! Jesus cried in anguish in the garden, "Father, if You are willing, remove this cup from Me" (Luke 22:42). But then He said the most important thing: "Yet not My will, but Yours be done." Jesus essentially said, "I am going to choose to trust You, Father, even though I feel a different way."

God understands that we don't always have the feeling of belief, and He knows that what He asks us to do doesn't always seem logical. But that doesn't really matter. If we know God is directing us, we can make a *choice* to believe and trust.

So how do we choose to believe, despite our feelings? We can apply a critical principle: Your feelings will follow your actions, not the other way around. Three steps to applying this principle will actually help change your feelings and help you "believe God and not your fear."

STEP 1: FOCUS ON WHATEVER IS LOVELY, AND THE FEELINGS OF PEACE WILL FOLLOW.

The first step is to choose to focus your thoughts on whatever is true and honorable. If you do, the feelings will follow. In Philippians 4:4 Paul said, "Rejoice in the Lord always; again I will say, rejoice!" When Paul wrote this, he was in prison—chained to a wall. How could Paul say "Rejoice!" when things were so tough? How can we? The answer comes in verses 8–9: "Fix your thoughts on what is true, and honorable, and right, and pure, and lovely, and admirable. Think about things that are excellent and worthy of praise. Keep putting into practice all you learned and received from me. . . . *Then the God of peace will be with you*" (NLT, emphasis added).

In our culture we tend to think that we feel a certain way so we act a certain way. If I don't *feel* it, I shouldn't have to *do* it. In fact, the way God created us is the reverse. Our feelings follow our actions. For example, think about the thirty-day Challenge with your man, mentioned in chapter 9. If you are annoyed at your husband and upset that he doesn't do this or that, and you tell him so, and you tell your girlfriends so, and you constantly pray for God to change him, do you think you will be more or less dissatisfied? But if you force yourself to set those thoughts aside and instead focus on what he does right—what is excellent and worthy of praise—and you tell him so, and you brag on those things to your girl-friends, and you thank God for those things in Him, what will you feel? You might just find your feelings about your husband changing.

In any challenging situation, once we focus on what is positive and choose to find contentment, our feelings will follow our focus. So eventually, we *want* to do the thing God is asking of us!

STEP 2: FIX YOUR EYES ON JESUS (NOT YOUR PROBLEM), AND YOUR FAITH WILL FOLLOW.

The second step of the principle that feelings follow actions is to keep your eyes on Jesus, not on what you need to believe Him about. When you do so, faith will follow. After the list of heroes of the faith in Hebrews 11, Hebrews 12 tells us to have the same kind of faith as they did. The next verse tells us how. "We do this by keeping our eyes on Jesus, the champion who initiates and perfects our faith" (Heb. 12:2 NLT).

Do not fix your eyes on all the things you are trying to believe God about: those are your problems! Do not fix your eyes on your fears, your worries, or your questions. Instead, fix your eyes on Jesus and His character.

When you see what God is asking of you and you fear, choose to tell yourself, *He is able. He is faithful.* When you worry or your thoughts go racing with all that could go wrong if you do what God asks, put on some worship music and turn your thoughts to Him, and remind yourself that Jesus is in control. God says *He* is the author of our faith, and when we doubt, He can strengthen our faith!

STEP 3: "FORGET NOT ALL HIS BENEFITS," AND YOUR BELIEF WILL FOLLOW.

The third step of this principle is to remind yourself of God's faithfulness to you in the past, and your tangible trust will follow. When you are faced with disappointment or difficulty, if you continually remind yourself of what amazing things the Lord has done for you before—if you remember, if you write them down, if you sing about them and talk about them—will it be easier or harder for you to trust that He has good things for you *this* time? It will definitely be easier.

David knew this. In Psalm 103:1–2 he said, "Praise the LORD, O my soul; all my inmost being, praise his holy name. Praise the LORD, O my soul, and forget not all his benefits" (NIV). Then David listed all the benefits the Lord gave him.

If you're having trouble trusting God in the present, remind yourself of what He has done for you in the past and praise Him for it! One of the best ways to do this is to keep a journal, recording your prayers and the answers to those prayers—recording the wonderful ways God has worked in your life. Or tell a friend the stories of God's faithfulness, and it will remind you, too!

When you apply these three steps and focus on the good and lovely things, when you focus on Jesus and not on your doubts, and when you remember what He has done for you in the past, you will find that, often, your fear will melt away, to be replaced by a settled peace that God is in control. As frail humans, we will probably never do this perfectly. But having the peace that passes all understanding will make our obedience to God's call much more simple. And that brings us to our final point.

Take Action

The final part of the biblical prescription for believing and trusting God is truly where the rubber meets the road. Once we know what God is asking (or have a sense of it) based on our relationship with Him, and once we make that decision to believe and trust, we have to take action. Just as we can *choose* to believe, trust, and remember what God has done, we have to make a choice to do something about it. And that choice has consequences. The children of Israel all too often said, "We believe!" but then they didn't take action based on it, and their belief withered and died.

Keep in mind that sometimes your action is to wait, which also takes a lot of trust. Other times your action is *not* to take action—or to prioritize your actions. Kim, in my core group, had the following advice for other single moms. "You don't have to do everything and be everything to everybody. You should make choices based on what pleases God first. If you go that route, it will all work out even if it doesn't look like it will."

The key is to realize that if we know we need to do something, we cannot wait until the fear is gone. And as we take a step of belief, not only will our feelings often follow, but often we will see the next step opening up in front of us.

Look at Joshua 3. It was time for the children of Israel to take possession of the Promised Land. It was time for hundreds of thousands of people and all their livestock to cross over the flood-stage Jordan River . . . with no bridge. It seemed impossible, yet, as commanded, they took the steps to do what they could do. Hundreds of thousands of people, tents, wagons, and livestock broke camp and headed to the river—probably with no clue how God would work this one out. And look what happened.

> So the people left their camp to cross the Jordan, and the priests who were carrying the Ark of the Covenant went ahead of them. It was the harvest season, and the Jordan was overflowing its banks. But as soon as the feet of the priests who were carrying the Ark touched the water at the river's edge, the water above that point began backing up a great distance away. . . . And the water below that point flowed on to the Dead Sea until the riverbed was dry. Then all the people crossed over near the town of Jericho. (Josh. 3:14–16 NLT)

It wasn't until the people actually *stepped* into the water that God moved. The same will often be true for us. We act, and God moves.

Trusting God

So what do *you* need to trust God for? If you feel like God is telling you to do something—to quit your job, to start a job again, to pick your kids up earlier, to adopt a child if you can't have your own, to change the way you're relating to your husband, or to take an evening off work each week so you can have some time to meet Christian single men. . . . Whatever it is, if you're scared, if you don't know how the Lord is going to accomplish that, don't try to figure it out! Instead, believe God and not your fear . . .

and step into the water. Simply take the next step, and watch and see what God does. Then you may see the next step opening up in front of you. Take that next step, and wait and watch, and you may see the next step and the next. And pretty soon, God has accomplished amazing things just because you took each step of obedience.

Stepping into an overflowing Jordan River is scary, but God is bigger than our fear. And if you are obeying Him, He has you by the hand. There is no *reason* to fear. Lucy, in my core group, shared what she learned about this throughout our sessions together. "My concern was that if I followed this biblical model I would miss out on something—that there's a catch somewhere. But what I've been learning is that as I trust God I can let go of some of that angst inside me that there's something I will miss out on. Granted, I'm a work in progress, but that's the path I've chosen to take. You can read the Word and know in your head about who God is, but when you're faced with a decision and have to *demonstrate* that you trust God, that's when you have to choose. Am I going to choose the world's way or God's way?"

Why not take a deep breath, choose God's way, and step into that river of life that your heavenly Father has led you to? No matter what that looks like, or what happens in life, God's way will always be the best way because it is His chosen path for you and His purposes.

12

Being God's Servant

*P*ast to present, the landscape of womanhood has included many history turners. These are women of uncommon influence who have changed the world by their unique imprint and left it a different place.

Esther was one such woman. When she was called from obscurity by a Persian king who needed a wife, her shrewdness and courage as his queen saved her fellow Jews from execution and extinction. Another history turner was Florence Nightingale. In an era when medicine was considered "man's work," Florence went against the grain and pursued a career in health care. Through hands-on involvement in wretched medical clinics and military infirmaries, she discovered that poor sanitary conditions were the root cause of many needless deaths. Today nurses and doctors all over the world trace their life-saving emphasis on sanitation to Ms. Nightingale. Then there was Rosa Parks, a courageous woman who took a front seat on an Alabama bus and changed the trajectory of America forever. There were many others: Susan B. Anthony, Margaret Mead, Emily Dickinson, Joan of Arc, Queen Elizabeth I, Harriet Beecher Stowe, Catherine the Great, Indira Gandhi, Cleopatra . . . the list goes on and on. History is full of women who have reshaped our world in one way or another. But no woman has turned history so significantly or as permanently as the first woman: Eve.

Eve's first claim to fame is simply that she was the mother of us all. Interestingly, biologists now believe this. Recent discoveries in genetics have led scientists to conclude that all humans are descendants of the same woman. The proof, they say, is in our shared mitochondrial DNA. In a *Time* magazine article titled "Everyone's Genealogical Mother," Michael Lemonick writes, "If family trees were charted indefinitely backward, they would eventually converge on a small group of ancients who were ancestors of us all. Now biologists suggest in a report to *Nature* that a single female living between 140,000 and 280,000 years ago in Africa was the ancestor of everyone on the earth today. Inevitably—and to the probable delight of creationists—many scientists are calling her 'Eve.'"[1]

Yes, Eve was a real person. Hard science is edging closer to the biblical plotline. And while DNA now offers us a genetic link to her, Genesis 3 offers us a much fuller picture. So take a look. No, you won't find her physically described there. You'll have to imagine that for yourself. But the social and spiritual images of Eve in Genesis 3 are eye-popping. These pictures have been purposefully preserved for us and for women of every generation to gain insight. Look closely enough at them, and you'll even notice traces of yourself in Eve. Yes, you are a unique individual, but at the same time, it's important to recognize your connectedness to your supragreat-grandmother and how she predisposes you as a woman to certain tendencies, traits, and temptations. That's why Eve is so important. Her past is our present.

Options

In Genesis 3 Eve discovered for the first time that there was something else in life besides God's will and calling for her. Life had options! Everything was not fixed or guaranteed. Choices could be made.

Offering one major option was a crafty serpent with an exceptional marketing strategy. As we mentioned in chapter 6, in the serpent's encounter with Eve, he pressed her from the outside to abandon those callings God had given her to embrace on the inside. And the emotional buttons this serpent pushed to tempt her in that direction should sound familiar to every modern woman.

- God and the man speaking for Him are holding you back. Don't you know that?
- You've been lied to.
- Do you call this fair—having these limitations placed on you?
- Can't you see how second-rate you are right now? Why are you doing this to yourself?
- It's time for you to take control of your own destiny and maximize your potential.
- You need to know that what you don't have is so much better than what you do have.
- Stop worrying; you won't die if you strike out on your own. You'll excel!
- Don't let others keep you from your best.
- You can have it all!

Theologians will tell you this serpent was actually only a puppet. Speaking through it was the master of all evil we know today as Satan. In the wonder of the original garden, a snake was certainly an appropriate disguise for Satan to use to approach and engage the first woman. In this agrarian setting it made sense. But to target modern women (and men), the puppets for marketing Satan's voice have had to change. Talk-show hosts, movie stars, college professors, advertising agencies, songwriters, authors, social critics, and even friends do nicely. These outlets are craftily manipulated and appropriately placed for maximum impact. But the messages themselves have not changed. Look at them again. Today's tempting voices use the same old Genesis 3 pickup lines. And every modern woman who listens to them becomes Eve all over again.

Satan's deception of Eve brought us to a cataclysmic moment that today still affects us all. Most of us know it simply as the fall. It was a moment when all of God's original intentions and Core Callings became twisted, distorted, and—most of all—difficult.

What the Fall Unleashed

Genesis 3 should have featured Adam in the starring role of a courageous protector. After all, he was supposed to head this relationship with the same loving, sacrificial leadership with which Jesus would later cover His church (Eph. 5:23). Instead, Adam was strangely missing from this dramatic scene as Eve dangerously entertained the serpent's overtures. Where was he? The tragedy is, he was actually around, though we will have to look closely in this moment to find him. After six long verses of satanic dialogue with Eve, we finally catch a brief glimpse of Adam. Almost as an afterthought, Genesis 3:6 says he was "with her." In other words, the whole time this evil madness was being unleashed on Eve, Adam was right there, watching his wife's strength wane as Satan deceived her into abandoning God's command not to eat the forbidden fruit.

Why does Adam abdicate his responsibility in this life-or-death moment? He should have snatched the fruit out of Eve's grasp and cut the head off that insidious, lying snake! Instead . . . he watched. As we discussed in chapter 4, one reason is the sinful passivity that emerges as Eve sinfully asserts her will and pushes back against God's commands. But we can guess that there may have been another devious factor at work as well.

Clearly, Adam was no dummy. He was an ingenious, creative, natural-born leader designed by God to rule the world. So he was keenly aware of what was happening and what was at stake. For those reasons it seems that Adam was also using the situation to test God, selfishly thinking, *I can't lose.* By letting his wife take the fruit without his direct involvement, Adam likely reasoned that he would win, regardless of the outcome. If she ate and died as God had previously warned (Gen. 2:17), he could profess innocence by not having participated. On the other hand, if Eve ate and didn't die, then Adam had proof that God was, in fact, holding back on what was best for them. In that case Adam still had time to join his wife in this new life. Obviously, Adam thought he had outwitted everyone, including God.

It was a huge mistake.

The truth is, as Adam stood and watched his wife entertain sin, *he* sinned! Adam denied God even before Eve's deception was complete.

He shunned his leadership responsibilities, he abandoned his wife, and he embraced evil in his heart. But rather than outwitting God, he discovered a higher reality he should have known: "God sees not as man sees, for man looks at the outward appearance, but the LORD looks at the heart" (1 Sam. 16:7).

And Eve, of course, wasn't just an innocent victim of events. She knew the rule—this *one* limit placed on them—but she freely and fully flouted it. As the conversation advanced with the serpent, it was clear to her that Satan was calling her to make a momentous decision that went contrary to her design and God's clear commands, and yet she continued to listen to that seductive voice.

And as we have seen, in the process she disregarded and disrespected her husband. Adam had told her God's restriction, but—with Adam standing right there!—she ignored it. Rather than looking to Adam and trusting him and his words, she essentially ignored not only God but also Adam's leadership and made the fateful choice *she* wanted to make. Then, after she ate, she turned to her husband and instructed him to do the same. Sensing that Eve had gotten away with it, Adam complied.

This was not just a "role reversal." Eve didn't "lead" and Adam become a "helper." No, in this tragic twisting of God's design, Eve took over, Adam checked out, . . . and the world fell. Spiritual death, not a better life, immediately descended on Eden, and humanity's relationship with God was severed.

Along with this separation from God, gender wounds were also unleashed on Adam and Eve and on their posterity. I (Robert) can tell you that in that crisis moment, authentic manhood became mangled. The negligent and selfish passivity Adam displayed in the garden now becomes the passivity of all men. Everywhere you look today, you see men take charge in sports, business, and politics. They are aggressive warriors when it comes to their personal pursuits.

But when it comes to social and spiritual responsibilities, all too often, passively standing there like the original Adam becomes more their norm. The wife waits for her man to lead at home, but after a while she falls into prodding him: "Let's go to church. When are you going to do something with the kids? What about our relationship? Where are we going in life? What are you going to do about _____ (fill in the blank)?" His response is the same as Adam's was to Eve: "You decide. You take over. You take the responsibility. I'll watch." In the substantive things of life—relational, social, and spiritual—men's sinful natural tendency is to be passive. It's their inheritance from Adam.

Authentic womanhood also took a major hit in the garden. My (Shaunti's) eyes have really been opened to just how much tragedy for women was unleashed that day. Eve lost her feminine nobility when she fell into Satan's deception. And just as Adam's passivity still lives in men today, Eve's vulnerability to deception still carries on in her daughters. In every generation women are enticed with the same forbidden fruit: to neglect, compromise, or abandon altogether God's callings—and His limits—for what the world convincingly promises us is better, more liberating . . . more "fair." If anything, the deceptive fruits of a modern world are more plentiful than ever before, and as women, we are naturally prone through Eve to take and eat. This is the inheritance Genesis says Eve leaves us—the tendency to believe that there is something better out there for us to pursue than what God has already prescribed and that we can manipulate things to have it our way. But it's all a painful lie.

Eve, who was promised so much by the serpent, was now left with a life of deep regret. Choosing to live from the outside in, she became *the* symbol of a failed and futile femininity for all women of every generation.

Nevertheless, she continues to have her followers. There are many thousands of them in every age. In fact, we all have that sinful seed within us. Whether big or small, there are those ways that we, like Eve, still secretly believe or act as if God's Core Callings can be short-changed or neglected in the pursuit of other, seemingly life-giving ambitions. Often, *helper* is not seen as a life-giving design that leads to the loving partnership we long for but as an antiquated concept whose time has past. Or children are essentially worked in around a career by women who still believe they can do it all. Talents are sidetracked on the seductive pursuit of keeping up with the Joneses instead of the urgent task of bringing light to darkness. The pursuit of worldliness—even unintentionally!—washes away authentic godliness and even common sense. As with the first Eve, today it is so easy for desires and delusions to dictate everything . . . and bring the same failures and heartaches.

So when faced with the seductive pull of this world, what will you do? What will *we* do? We will be wise. We will learn from Eve and not repeat her mistakes. We will enjoy the opportunities our modern world offers but never at the expense of God's Core Callings on our lives. We will choose to live courageously from the inside out. We live as a "new Eve." And as we mentioned in chapter 4, God has given us a great role model as a new Eve: Mary, the mother of Jesus.

Mary: Eve's Righteous Twin

Unlike the original Eve, Mary is a model of womanhood we can follow. The more I (Shaunti) have studied the life of Mary, the more I have realized just what a shame it is that we don't study her more. We certainly spend a lot of time trying not to be like Eve, but how much better it is to also have Mary as someone we can emulate.

Some Christians almost want to downplay Mary's importance as a role model simply because we have seen other believers have an excessive reverence toward her. But just because some go too far, that should not keep us from learning what we can from the example of her life. After all, God looked down on the whole human race and handpicked this woman to be His mother! If God selected her in that way, we need to respect that He had a great reason and learn all we can from her life, especially as her story compares to Eve's.

And as you will see, it relates to *everything* we have been talking about throughout this book. We all want to be the "new Eve" as opposed to the old one.

In chapter 4, we briefly compared Eve and Mary in our discussion of biblical womanhood. First, we saw that Mary and Eve were both offered the chance to accept or reject God's Word. Eve shunned God's Word,

> We all want to be the "new Eve" as opposed to the old one.

but Mary embraced it. Second, we saw that Eve rejected God's callings, but Mary fulfilled them. And third, we learned that while both women expected good to come of their choices, only Mary actually received the blessing.

Mary's godly choice also brought her suffering. As most other godly men and women have found, obedience provides no automatic escape from the difficulty of this dark world. But Mary's trials could never offset the deep joy and long-term, eternal blessing she received. How small and insignificant her tribulations must have seemed once she held the King of kings as a tiny baby in her arms, followed him around as a toddler, and watched him grow into the most extraordinary man who ever lived.

> God's blessing on Mary's life came not because she *tried* to have blessing, but because she put her life completely at God's disposal and said, "I'm yours." ॐ

Mary's choice was used to bring the giver of new life to all mankind, for every generation to come. Her choice brought blessing. And God's blessing on her life came not because she *tried* to have blessing—that was what Eve did—but *because she was willing to put herself and her life and her expectations completely at God's disposal* and say, essentially, "I'm Yours."

Mary's Choices / Our Choices

I think all of us want to be like Mary. We want to be able to have great outcomes, not regrets. But we also know it is so hard sometimes. So what enabled Mary able to make such a hard choice and stick with it?

First, she knew what any of us can learn—in fact, she knew the things we *have* been learning in this book. She followed her Core Callings. And even though she may not have realized it, she embraced all of the Faith Steps we must take to follow God's compass and navigate through life as women.

Second, Mary knew and accepted one awesome fact: it's not about me; it's about Him.

In an early Life Ready core group session, we really wrestled with the truths of what God asks of us. We had been talking through the idea of the Core Callings and what they mean for us. We had some great discussions about marriage, singleness, motherhood, career, and all of the other issues we've talked about in this book. Julia, the youngest in our group, sat quietly through much of the discussion. Then near the end she said something like this, "We've been talking about 'my skills,' 'my questions,' 'my career,' 'my kids,' and so on. But we have to realize: it's not about me. It's about Him and His purposes. We've given our lives to God. He's our Master, and He can do what He wants with our lives." There was dead quiet, and then I said, "The twenty-five-year-old said the wisest thing the whole night." We all laughed, but then Lucy quietly spoke up, and we could hear the conviction in her voice. "I can get behind that. I can. That is clear. That is the answer. I can do that."

When we were talking about it later, Sally shared a vital comment from her perspective as a stay-at-home mom. She said, "I have learned 'it's not about me' daily with two-year-old twins and a five-year-old. Kids have a way of reminding us of that." We were reminded of the broadcasting career she had set aside as she continued, "If it *is* about me, then I'm wasting my time. But if it's *not* about me, then I'm investing in the next generation and loving my neighbor more than myself."

Two thousand years ago an angel came to Mary and told her that she had a calling many would view as impossibly difficult. When the angel said, "This is what God wants of you," what did she reply? "I am the Lord's servant" (Luke 1:38 NIV). In other words, "It's not about me and my wishes for my life. He is the Potter, I am the clay. He is the Master, I am the servant. And I am at His service; I want what *He* wants for me."

A few verses later we read that when her cousin Elizabeth saw Mary for the first time after that momentous choice, Elizabeth's child leapt in her womb, and she cried out to Mary: "Blessed are you among women! . . . Blessed is she who has believed that what the Lord has said to her will be accomplished!" (Luke 1:42, 45 NIV). She's saying, "Wow, Mary, *you* are *blessed!*" But look at Mary's response:

> And Mary said: *"My soul glorifies the* Lord *and my spirit rejoices in* God *my Savior, for* he *has been mindful of the humble state of his servant. From now on all generations will call me blessed, for the Mighty One has done great things for me—holy is* his *name.* His *mercy extends to those who fear him, from generation to generation.* He *has performed mighty deeds with his arm;* he *has scattered those who are proud in their inmost thoughts.* He *has brought down rulers from their thrones but has lifted up the humble.* He *has filled the hungry with good things but has sent the rich away empty.* He *has helped his servant Israel, remembering to be merciful to Abraham and his descendants forever, even as he said to our fathers. (Luke 1:46–55 NIV, author emphasis)*

So when Elizabeth said, "Mary *you* are so blessed," Mary's immediate response was, "It's not about me. It's about God. He is fulfilling thousands of years of His promises to His nation. He has done all these things. He has a plan He is carrying out. I am simply being His humble servant."

It's not about me.

When you get scared about what will happen to your skills if you leave the workforce for five or ten years, . . . it's not about you. It's about God's big-picture purpose for that time of shepherding your children well.

When you get upset that you're doing your part but your husband isn't doing his, . . . it's not about you. It's about God using you to reach out to your man and provide an example to the world.

If you're single and lonely and frustrated that you don't have the companion your heart is longing for, . . . it's not about you. It's about looking at where God has you at this moment and saying, "What are *Your* purposes for this time in my life, Lord?"

When you are loving your volunteer ministry at that inner-city tutoring program but *really* don't feel like fighting traffic to get there when you're tired, . . . it's not about you. It's about being the hands and feet of Jesus to a hurting world.

In all of these things, *God is the Potter; we are the clay* (Isa. 64:8). He will use us to advance His purpose, but it is not *about* us. And, of course, the key is this: He will use us to advance His purposes to every degree that we will let Him.

Two thousand years ago, Mary stared at the angel, took a deep breath, and said something that changes everything: "I am the Lord's servant. . . . May it be to me as you have said" (Luke 1:38 NIV).

Ladies, it is time for us to take these steps of faith. We need to be clear about our lives, bold in our faith, and able to find God's best. We all want to thrive in this do-it-all world and reach the end of this earthly life with satisfaction instead of regrets. We want a family that loves and honors us. We want to be used by God to make an impact on our family and our world and pass down something precious from generation to generation. We want to be God's servant.

Mary was like that. And we can be too. "Lord, may it be to me as you have said."

$\mathcal{N}otes$

Chapter 1

1. Douglas B. Sosnik, Matthew J. Dowd, and Ron Fournier, *Applebee's America: How Successful Political, Business, and Religious Leaders Connect with the New American Community* (New York: Simon and Schuster, 2006), 224.

2. Celinda Lake and Kellyanne Conway, *What Women Really Want: How American Women Are Quietly Erasing Political, Racial, Class, and Religious Lines to Change the Way We Live* (New York: Free Press, 2005), 2–3.

3. See www.bls.gov/opub/ted/2000/feb/wk3/art03.htm.

4. Belinda Luscombe, "Workplace Salaries: At Last Women on Top," *Time*, 1 September 2010.

5. Ibid., and Bureau of Labor Statistics (Table 5. Employment status of the population by sex, marital status, and presence and age of own children under 18, 2008–09 annual averages, http://data.bls.gov/cgi-bin/print.pl/news.release/famee.t05.htm).

6. Cover article in *The Atlantic*, "The End of Men" (July–August 2010).

7. Center for Women's Business Research, "Key Facts about Women Owned Businesses, 2008–2009 Update," www.womensbusinessresearchcenter.org/research/keyfacts.

8. "The Bottom Line: Corporate Performance and Women's Representation on Boards," *Catalyst*, 2007, http://catalyst.org/publication/2007/the-bottom-line-corporate-performance-and-womens-representation-on-boards.

9. See "Women Are the Backbone of the Christian Congregations in America," the Barna Group, 6 May 2000.

10. Michelle Conlin, "The New Gender Gap: From Kindergarten to Grad School, Boys Are Becoming the Second Sex," *BusinessWeek*, 26 May 2003.

11. U.S. Census Bureau, "School Enrollment in the United States," Current Population Survey, October 2008.

12. "The Growing Gender Gaps in College Enrollment and Degree Attainment in the U.S. and Their Potential Economic and Social Consequences," a study prepared by the Center for Labor Market Studies at Northeastern University, May 2003.

13. Tamar Lewin, "At Colleges, Women Are Leaving Men in the Dust," *New York Times*, 9 July 2006.

14. "The Condition of Education," a 379-page report of federal statistics, 1 June 2006.

15. Hanna Rosin, "The End of Man," *The Atlantic* (July–August, 2010).

16. National Center for Education Statistics, http://nces.ed.gov/fastfacts/display.asp?id=72.

17. Obtained from the Association to Advance Collegiate Schools of Business and *The Detroit News*, "Female MBA Students . . . ," 29 July 2004.

18. Galinsky, et al., "Times Are Changing."

19. Peg Tyre, "The Trouble with Boys," *Newsweek*, 30 January 2006.

20. Will Durant, *Caesar and Christ* (New York: MJF Books, 1944) is the source for most of the information on women's roles and rights in middle and late Rome. On the dramatic increase in divorce, sanctioned adultery, and abortion, see 134, 211, and 396. On the unpopularity of maternity, see 222. On women becoming doctors, lawyers, gladiators, and professionals of every sort, see 370.

21. Ibid., 438.

22. Shaunti Feldhahn, *The Male Factor* (New York: Crown Business, 2009), 283.

23. Caitlin Flanagan, *To Hell with All That: Loving and Loathing Our Inner Housewife* (New York: Little, Brown, 2006), xvii.

24. Maria Shriver, *Ten Things I Wish I'd Known—Before I Went Out into the Real World* (New York: Warner, 2000), 61, 71.

25. Joanne Kaufman, "Rachael Ray's Recipe for Joy," *Good Housekeeping*, August 2006.

26. "Census: More Women Childless Than Ever Before," AP, 25 October 2003.

27. Cari Tuna and Joann S. Lublin, "Welch: 'No such Thing as Work-Life Balance,'" *The Wall Street Journal*, 14 July 2009.

28. Sylvia Ann Hewlett, *Creating a Life: Professional Women and the Quest for Children* (New York: Talk Miramax Books, 2002), 3.

29. Transcript, *Oprah*, 16 January 2002.

Chapter 2

1. Dr. Edward Diener, in Marilyn Elias, "Psychologists Know What Makes People Happy," *USA Today*, 10 December 2002. Dr. Diener is a psychologist at the University of Illinois.

2. Dr. William Sheldon, cited by Huston Smith, *Why Religion Matters: The Fate of the Human Spirit in an Age of Disbelief* (San Francisco: HarperSanFrancisco, 2001), 26.

Chapter 3

1. No source available.

2. Transcript, *Oprah*, 16 January 2002.

3. Carolyn Heilbrun, *Reinventing Womanhood* (New York: W. W. Norton, 1979), 196.

4. U.S. Census Bureau, "Parents and Children in Stay-at-Home Parent Family Groups: 1994 to Present," Current Population Survey 2003.

5. U.S. Census Bureau, "Census Bureau Reports Families with Children Increasingly Face Unemployment," press release, 15 January 2010.

6. Vicki Courtney, *5 Conversations You Must Have with Your Daughter* (Nashville: B&H, 2008), 179–80.

7. Linda Hirshman, "Unleashing the Wrath of Stay-at-Home Moms," *Washington Post*, sec. B-1, 18 June 2006.

8. Courtney, *5 Conversations You Must Have with Your Daughter,* 219.

9. Stephanie Coontz, *Marriage, a History: From Obedience to Intimacy, or How Love Conquered Marriage* (New York: Viking, 2005), 4.

10. David Brooks, *On Paradise Drive: How We Live Now (and Always Have) in the Future Tense* (New York: Simon and Schuster, 2004), 171.

11. U.S. Census Bureau, "Births to Teens and Unmarried Mothers and Births with Low Birth Weight by Race and Hispanic Origin: 1990 to 2007."

12. Debra Rosenberg and Pat Wingert, "First Comes Junior in a Baby Carriage," *Newsweek*, 4 December 2006, 56.

13. Anne Kingston, *The Meaning of Wife: A Provocative Look at Women and Marriage in the Twenty-first Century* (New York: Farrar, Straus and Giroux, 2004), 1.

14. Kim Parker, "The Harried Life of the Working Mother," Pew Research Center, 1 October 2009, http://pewsocialtrends.org/pubs/745/the-harried-life-of-the-working-mother. See also "Women Desire a Balance between Career and Family," *PRNewswire*, 5 September 2000.

15. U.S. Census Bureau, "Labor Force Participation Among Mothers 15 to 44 Years Old by Fertility Status and Selected Characteristics," Current Population Survey, June 2006.

16. U.S. National Center for Health Statistics, "Live Births, Deaths, Marriages, and Divorces: 1960 to 2007," *Vital Statistics of the United States,* and *National Vital Statistics Reports* (www.cdc.gov/nchs/nvss.htm).

17. Peter Drucker, "Managing Knowledge Means Managing Oneself," *Leader to Leader,* 16, Spring 2000.

18. Pamela Norris, *Eve: A Biography* (New York: New York University Press, 1999), 402.

Chapter 4

1. Francis Brown, S. R. Driver, and C. A. Briggs, *A Hebrew and English Lexicon of the Old Testament* (Oxford: Oxford University Press, 1968).

Chapter 5

1. George Barna, *The Future of the American Family* (Chicago: Moody Press, 1993), 121.

2. John Stott, *Decisive Issues Facing Christians Today* (Old Tappan, NJ: Revell, 1990), 120.

3. Stephen B. Clark, *Man and Woman in Christ* (East Lansing, MI: Tabor Publications, 1980).

Chapter 6

1. Drawn from a Ken Boa sermon given at Dunwoody Community Church, Dunwoody, Georgia, March 2010.

2. Lisa Bergren and Rebecca Price, *What Women Want: The Life You Crave and How God Satisfies* (New York: WaterBrook Press, 2007).

Chapter 7

1. "Hooking Up, Hanging Out, and Hoping for Mr. Right: College Women on Mating and Dating Today. An Institute for American Values Report to the Independent Women's Forum," http://www.americanvalues.org/html/a-pr_hooking_up.html.

2. Sylvia Ann Hewlett, *Creating a Life: Professional Women and the Quest for Children* (New York: Talk Mirimax Books, 2002), 89.

3. Adapted from Hewlett, 301–2.

4. See www.brainyquote.com.

5. The reality that regular worship attendance reduces divorce rates by 35 percent or more has been demonstrated in separate university studies conducted and/or analyzed independent of each other as noted below. Due to misinterpretation of a George Barna study, there is a common misconception among churchgoers that the rate of divorce is the same in the church as in general society, which is not the case. George Barna's poll designated someone a "Christian" based on a poll about what they said they believed and did not ask about their religious practices such as actually going to church—which, as noted, is correlated with at least a one-third reduction in divorce rates. For more information, see analysis and studies done by Dr. Brad Wilcox at the University of Virginia (see http://center.americanvalues.org/pdf_dl.php?name=researchbrief11) and by

Dr. Annette Mahoney at Bowling Green State University. See also Stan Guthrie's interview with Brad Wilcox in *Christianity Today*, "What Married Women Want," October 2006, 122. For additional analysis, see the Focus on the Family article, "The Role Faith Plays in Marriage and the Likelihood of Divorce," by Glenn Stanton, http://www.citizenlink.org/FOSI/marriage/divorce/A000000901.cfm.

6. "Hardwired to Connect." Purchasing information can be found online (http://www.americanvalues.org) or from the Institute for American Values; 1841 Broadway, Suite 211; New York, NY 10023.

7. From an NPR report by Vicky Que, 22 September 2003. The report can be accessed at http://www.npr.org/templates/story/story.php?storyId=1438731.

Chapter 8

1. Philippe Ariès, trans. Patricia M. Ranum, *Western Attitudes toward Death: From the Middle Ages to the Present* (Baltimore: Johns Hopkins University Press, 1974), 92.

2. National Center for Policy Analysis, November 2003, http://www.ncpa.org/pub/st/st264/.

3. Joan Didion, *The Year of Magical Thinking* (New York: Random House, 2005).

4. Summary provided via e-mail to Shaunti Feldhahn by Andy Stanley's assistant about the book [Andy Stanley, *Choosing to Cheat* (Sisters, OR: Multnomah, 2003)].

Chapter 9

1. See http://abcnews.go.com/US/story?id=91890&page=1.

2. Christopher Andersen, *The Day John Died* (New York: William Morrow, 2000), 32.

3. George Gilder, *Men and Marriage* (Gretna, LA: Pelican Publishing, 1993), 10.

4. Willard F. Harley Jr., *His Needs, Her Needs: Building an Affair-Proof Marriage* (Grand Rapids, MI: Revell, 1994), 77.

5. Will Durant, *Caesar and Christ* (New York: MJF Books, 1944), 370.

6. Jeff and Shaunti Feldhahn and Eric and Lisa Rice, *For Young Men Only* and *For Young Women Only* (Sisters, OR: Multnomah Publishers, 2006).

7. Harley, *His Needs, Her Needs,* 43–44.

Chapter 10

1. The 1990 movie *Awakenings,* is based on the real-life story of neurologist Oliver Sacks who in 1969 discovered that a new drug would awaken catatonic patients who survived an encephalitis epidemic from years earlier. While this

storyline provides a great metaphor for our purposes, we should note that we are not endorsing the movie itself, especially as the film seems to endorse the use of a Ouija board, which is one type of divination and witchcraft—something God prohibits in the strongest possible terms.

2. Colin Welland, *Chariots of Fire* (Warner Bros., 1981).

3. Frederick Buechner, *Wishful Thinking: A Seeker's ABC* (San Francisco: Harper San Francisco, 1993), 119.

Chapter 11

1. Angelo Pizzo, *Rudy* (TriStar Pictures, 1993).

Chapter 12

1. Michael Lemonick, "Everyone's Genealogical Mother," *Time*, 26 January 1987.

Acknowledgments

From Shaunti

Working with a respected leader like Robert Lewis has been one of the great professional experiences of my life. I have learned so much from him, not only from his many years of wisdom as a pastor and leader but from his humility. Far from being territorial about this message, he has fully and willingly allowed me to change and build on a vision and a book (*The New Eve*) that he developed and poured himself into for years. His selflessness and kingdom focus are inspiring and profoundly challenging to me. I don't know that I yet have maturity or grace to hand over what I think of as "my" work to someone else in that way, and I'm immensely grateful to Robert for showing me by example that it is not "my" work at all and that I can trust the true Author with open hands.

I also know that this message would not have been advanced if adding to it were just up to me. I'm grateful to the core group of women who walked the road with me for a year or more as we wrestled with further developing a biblical vision that would help and apply to women of every life stage and background. To Angie, Ann, Dawn, Debbie, Ginger, Jill, Julia, Kim R., Kim W., Leslie, Lucy, Sally, and Wendy: thank you for linking arms with me and accompanying me so willingly on this journey! I pray this was a key step in your own journey to finding God's best for your life!

I also thank Roswell Assembly of God and the many women who cheerfully gathered there every week to go through the "pilot version" of the *Life Ready* study and provide such willing feedback and insight along the way.

Working with B&H Publishing Group for the first time has been delightful, particularly due to the vision, guidance, and immense patience of Jennifer Lyell. My deep appreciation goes out to Dana Wilkerson for her insight, skill, and enviable ability to translate some often-vague phone instructions, a dozen different videos, and rapid-fire e-mails from two different authors into easy-to-read text! Similar thanks goes out to Jeremy Howard for his original work on *The New Eve*.

Writing any book would be absolutely impossible without my staff team, and the team is usually doing everything *else* to lighten my load so I can write. But in this case I am delighted and grateful that several of these women—Leslie Hettenbach, Karen Newby, and Julia Wright—became integrally involved in developing the actual content by participating in my core group, organizing the first Life Ready study group, and providing key input into message and format. I am grateful for a new friend, Cheryl Baker, who so willingly dug into the "womanhood Scriptures" to advance this project. My deep thanks also, as always, to my staff director Linda Crews, who keeps everything running, Tally Whitehead, and all the others who use their considerable talents for God's kingdom purposes! This also applies to my amazing prayer team, who are so faithful to pray for anointing, wisdom, protection, productivity—and many other things—every step of the way.

Finally, to my two little squirts and my amazing husband, Jeff: I delight in you and am so grateful to you. Experiencing your life and being loved by you are primary ways I feel the Father's love for me. And it is to that heavenly Father, the Audience of One, that I gratefully dedicate it all.

From Robert

Every book I've written starts first with a big thank-you to my wife Sherard. I have never met a more consistent "life ready woman" than you sweetie! You are priceless . . . and always have been.

A special thanks to my wonderful daughters, Elizabeth James and Rebekah Lewis. Both of you put in countless hours reading specific chapters and talking out with me various ideas and concepts. You both made a real difference in this book.

Jeremy Howard's contribution was huge. Without Jeremy's energetic spirit, superb professionalism, and writing help, this book would never have found its way into print. It was a privilege working with you.

Dr. Margaret Feurtado graciously took the lead in holding up this project in prayer. She continues to do so even now, and how grateful and blessed Shaunti and I are for that. Thank you, Margaret.

The FBC prayer team in Little Rock also deserves special recognition for their ongoing prayer support. Thank you so much ladies.

I would also like to thank Jennifer Lyell at B&H for stepping in and believing in this project. Your quick action made this book become a reality, and for that I am extremely grateful. Thank you, Jennifer. It's been a pleasure working with you and the B&H team.

Finally, I am grateful to God that He brought Shaunti and I together. Originally Shaunti graciously gave advice and support for my original book. But honestly, it lacked the insights and applications only a woman with Shaunti's experience could provide. When I extended to her the offer of partnering with me on a much better and more balanced remake, she not only consented, but did so with heart and soul.

Thank you, Shaunti, for all your hard work and faithfulness. You are an extremely gifted woman! I truly believe your contributions have made this work something that women everywhere will find life-changing. To God be the glory!

the LIFE READY woman

The difference between "doing it all" and doing what matters

No matter what your life looks like, God has an individual mission and plan that He's carefully designed. And He wants you to find it.

The Life Ready Woman Video Series helps every woman discover God's biblical roadmap for finding balance, peace, and delight in this crazy, contemporary life. Speaker, best-selling author, wife, and mother Shaunti Feldhahn unfurls God's plan and purposes for women. She hones in on the practical implications for each individual woman: exploring her heart, her relationships, and her unique makeup.

This study equips you to:

- experience more of life—with less regret
- minimize stress
- find clear, courageous direction about God's priorities for *you*
- bring a biblical balance to life (family, work, church, relationships, activities . . .)
- discover clarity in relationships, including with God and men
- (finally) enjoy more rest